A
Witness
Primer

A
Witness
Primer

Erwin J. Kolb

Publishing House
St. Louis

Copyright © 1986 Concordia Publishing House
3558 S. Jefferson Avenue, St. Louis, MO 63118-3968
Manufactured in the United States of America

Library of Congress Cataloging-in-Publication Data

Kolb, Erwin J.
    A witness primer.

    1. Witness bearing (Christianity) I. Title.
BV4520.K64   1986   248'.5   86-12902
ISBN 0-570-04441-3

1 2 3 4 5 6 7 8 9 10 IB 95 94 93 92 91 90 89 88 87 86

This book is dedicated to all the participants of Lay Evangelism Workshops and Witness Workshops and to the students in the Ambassador for Christ Program at Concordia College, Seward, Nebraska, who helped me grow in my witnessing.

Contents

Acknowledgments —

A book like this one is never the product of one person. Many individuals have contributed ideas and thoughts through the years that were absorbed, used, modified, and so assimilated that their individual source is no longer recognized. I wish to acknowledge my appreciation to all those who have helped shape my understanding and practice of witnessing, great leaders in the church such as Elmer Kettner, Herman Gockel, Oswald Waech, Theodore Raedeke, W. Leroy Biesenthal, many others, and the participants of my workshops.

Acknowledgments are made of those who read this manuscript in the first draft and made significant contribution to the final draft through their critiques and suggestions: Lyle Muller, W. Leroy Biesenthal, Oswald Waech, Ralph Geisler, Bruce Lieske, Richard Bimler, and Jane Fryar. Thanks are given to faithful and efficient secretaries Cathy Cook and Helen Matthews.

Finally, I want to acknowledge the support of my wife, Bernice, who patiently allowed me to "hide out" in my study as I worked on this book.

Introduction

"Last year I went to New Orleans for our company's annual sales convention. After dinner, three of us went for a walk and ran into a sidewalk preacher. You never heard such shouting, haranguing, and wild predictions. It really turned me off. I was cringing inside. The two guys I was with were cracking jokes about the fellow and religion in general. I was really mad at the sidewalk preacher for being such an easy target, and I was angry with myself for lacking the guts and knowledge to defend my faith. I didn't want to defend him, because ranting and raving isn't what Christianity is all about. But I thought, *what if one of my friends asks me what it is all about? I don't think I can explain it.*"[1]

That's Peter's own story. And Peter is not just an unchurched skeptic, nor an interested moralist. You would call him an "upstanding Christian"! He is married and the father of two children. He goes to church regularly and is involved in serving on boards and committees and pitching in whenever there is work to be done at church. He even takes part in the congregation's program of visitation to shut-ins and the hospitalized.

But when Peter is with his unchurched associates and religion is ridiculed, what does he say? Most Christians at one time or another find themselves in situations like Peter's, and most are as mute as Peter was. It's not that Peter didn't want to explain what Christianity is all about, or even to share what he himself believed, but he is filled with inhibitions and fears that make him hesitate and clam up. So he finds some comfort in saying "I'm not really big on talking about my religion . . . I don't believe in pushing my faith down anyone's throat." But he sometimes feels guilt and wonders, "Am I less of a Christian because I don't talk about it?"

Can Peter be helped? Can he learn to understand the reasons why he does not talk about his faith to his friends? Can he learn some ways to begin to broach the subject? Can he develop some skills in explaining Christianity and giving his own personal witness?

I believe he can, and that is the reason for this book. Yes, it is another book on evangelism and, since evangelism books have been so popular among publishers in recent years, some will likely ask, "Who needs another book on evangelism?" I say Peter does! And so do all the Peters and the Pearls who feel guilty for not giving the Christian witness they earnestly want to give. Then there are those who "do evangelism" in their own way and find it difficult or often feel very uncomfortable about it. Finally, there are some who "witness" in such a way that they give offense and drive more people away from the Christian faith than they draw to it.

So the purpose of this book is to help Christians witness to Jesus Christ in a winsome way, a way that brings joy to them and draws others to Christ through their witness. It is to help Christians fulfill their role as the witness Jesus said all His followers are, "You shall be My witnesses" (Acts 1:8) and to help them do what the apostle Peter says: "Be ready at all times to answer anyone who asks you to explain the hope you have in you, but do it with gentleness and respect" (1 Peter 3:15–16 TEV).

A Witness Primer uses the same basic approach as *A Prayer Primer*. Some people understood that title to mean a "primer" as a book, according to the dictionary definition:

Primer: A small book of elementary principles, such as a beginning book for teaching children to read.

Others read the title word "prime-r," spelled the same way as primer, but meaning "that which primes."

Like *A Prayer Primer*, this book is intended to be both, a book of elementary principles about witnessing and a book that primes in the sense that it helps motivate Christians to witness and guides them in their continuing witness.

This book follows an acrostic built on the word *witness*, with the hope that this acrostic can help the reader summarize and remember the content of the book and then put it into practice:

W for *Witness*—what it means to witness and how to start doing it

I for *Intentional*—taking the initiative

T for *Testimony*—a personal witness together with the objective witness

N for *Natural*—rather than a programmed witness

E for *Everyone*—each disciple of Jesus Christ is a witness

S for *Saved*—by God's grace through faith in Jesus Christ

S for *Some*—the Lord adds to the church those who are being saved (see Acts 2:47). Some reject, but some are saved, and we rejoice when they are saved (1 Cor. 9:22; Acts 8:39).

It is my prayer that *A Witness Primer* will be for you both a primer and a prime-r.

1. W for Witness ____

"We were visiting in this home, somewhat run-down and cluttered, talking to a young mother, with six children running around the room. My partner and I ran out of things to say so I just blurted out, 'We just want you to know that God loves you.' At this the young lady of the house became upset and lashed out at us, 'How can you say that? Look around you! If God loves me, why does He let me live like this?' "

This was the experience an evangelism caller described one evening in a meeting at St. Matthew Lutheran Church, St. Louis, Missouri. Several of us had been invited to the meeting in order to help the Evangelism Committee evaluate its program and the work of its callers. "What should we have said?" was her question. "We didn't know what to say, so we got out of there as quickly as we could," she went on. "But then we were despondent because we felt that we had failed."

A Witness Is Not . . .

We discussed at length what she could have said. We discovered that the problem was in understanding what a Christian witness does and does not do. A Christian witness does not supply all the answers, or solve everyone's problems. The callers in that home in north St. Louis could never give an answer that could satisfy that mother as to why she had to live on ADC and try to raise her children in such poor conditions. But the witnesses could give a witness in that situation. We agreed that the callers could have said:

"I don't know why God let's you live like this, but I do know that when I have difficult times or problems to deal with, it helps me to know that God loves me and will help me deal with my problems."

A witness is not an answer giver or problem solver. When Peter said that we must always be ready to give an answer, he does not say, give an answer to everybody's questions about religious philosophy, about the economic or political problems of

15

the world, or about hunger and poverty. He says that we must be ready to explain why we have hope, why we can deal with those problems through our faith in the love and providence of an almighty God and our Savior Jesus Christ (2 Peter 3:15–16).

Notice also that Peter did not say that we must know all of the Scripture and be able to quote passages, as good as that often is, nor that we must know the whole body of Christian doctrine. Peter's emphasis is for us to answer by telling others what we believe, why we believe, and how this affects our lives to give us hope in the face of every difficulty. What we believe is of course based on the Scriptures and sometimes we do quote passages to share what we believe, but the emphasis in witnessing is on the personal testimony.

At a Witness Workshop in St. Louis a lay minister in one of the congregations explained the problem they had with their evangelism program. "We tried for years to get members to make evangelism calls, but we were teaching them to expect to get a response when they made a call and they became discouraged when they didn't get results. In fact, disappointed callers often gave up all witnessing because they thought they ought to see people come to church and to faith immediately following this witness."

A witness is not a converter. Only God can convert people and only "some" are converted as a result of a witness, as will be discussed in other chapters. Bringing people to faith in Jesus as Savior and Lord is the goal of all Christian witnessing and evangelism but it is not the responsibility of the witness. God does it in His own time and in His own way as He uses the witness of many people. He used the apostle Paul, who said that God made His appeal "through us. We beseech you on behalf of Christ, be reconciled to God" (2 Cor. 5:20). As God used His apostle Paul to plead with people to "be reconciled to God" so today he also uses human beings to deliver the "message of reconciliation" (2 Cor. 5:19). That is the task of those whom He calls to the office of public ministry as well as the lay people they equip and motivate.

Church Growth studies suggest that a person on the average hears the Gospel seven times in different ways before that person is ready to believe it. If you invite your neighbor to attend church with you, don't give up when he declines the first invitation. Expect to invite him at least seven times! When you witness to a friend, he may not believe your Gospel message immediately. Let God do His work as He chooses. You continue to do yours as His witness.

A Witness Is a Disciple of Jesus Christ

A witness is a disciple of Jesus Christ. A disciple is a follower and one who learns from a respected teacher. The New Testament speaks about disciples of Jesus Christ as those whom Jesus has called and brought into a personal relationship with Himself. The disciple not only learns from His Master, Jesus, but he follows His example, imitates Him, and tries to become like Him.

Just before Jesus returned to heaven, having accomplished His mission of reconciling the world to His Father in heaven, He said to His disciples, "You shall receive power when the Holy Spirit has come upon you; and you shall be My witnesses in Jerusalem and in all Judea and Samaria and to the end of the earth" (Acts 1:8). He used a Greek word for witness that is commonly used in the New Testament, *martus*. Our English word *martyr* comes from that Greek word. While the word in the New Testament has a legal flavor like a person on a witness stand telling the facts of what he has seen or heard, its meaning was broadened. It came to mean also one who stood up for a cause so consistently and strongly that he was willing to give his life for the cause. His death was his witness, the ultimate demonstration of his conviction, and thus he was a "martyr."

In the New Testament the word *martus* is used over 300 times and many more times with compounds or prefixes added for emphasis, such as, "witnessing with," "witnessing against" or "witnessing earnestly." As Jesus left the earth, His plan for continuing His work was that His followers would tell others and thus the message would spread, like ripples of water when one throws a stone in a lake. The message would spread from Jerusalem out to the surrounding province in Judea and then to the next province, Samaria, and out to the ends of the world.

The first witnesses, the disciples to whom Jesus spoke in Acts 1:8, actually saw Jesus in the flesh, and they could witness in a very literal sense. They said to the Sanhedrin, which tried to stop them from witnessing, "We cannot but speak of what we have seen and heard" (Acts 4:20). Other followers, or disciples, of Jesus Christ heard the message from the apostles, and they told what they had "seen and heard" through the apostles. Today we who are disciples of Jesus Christ tell what we have "seen and heard." We share both the objective facts of Jesus' life, death, and resurrection as we have learned them from the Scriptures, and we share our experiences of what faith in Him means in our personal lives. The first witnesses, the apostles, were witnesses in a *literal* sense of the word, while we are witnesses in an *extended* sense of the word.

A Witness Shares the Good News of Jesus Christ

History includes a long list of Christian martyrs who witnessed by their death. One of the most moving and impressive accounts is that of Perpetua, a young married woman with a baby in her arms, and Felicity, a slave girl who gave birth to a daughter while in prison. Pagan friends and relatives urged the two young women to deny their faith and thus save their lives. They refused. A detailed account tells how they helped each other when thrown to wild beasts in the arena with three male martyrs. They survived the wild beasts, and a gladiator was sent to kill them. All five exchanged a kiss of peace with promises of an immediate reunion with Christ in heaven. The two babies were brought up by fellow Christians.

When you read that story, what impresses you? To what did their martyrdom give witness? To their heroism? their stubbornness? their faith? the cruelty of the Romans? In reading the history of the Christian martyrs it is easy to focus our feeling of sympathy and even our respect and admiration on the martyrs. We easily overlook the One who is at the center of the reason for their death, Jesus Christ. The same can happen in the witness that Christians give today by their lives and their words of testimony. The hearer may be impressed by the witness but not confront the person of Christ. A witness points people, not to oneself, but to Jesus Christ. A witness shares the Good News that Jesus Christ offers new life and peace to everyone.

Our English word *evangelism* comes from the Greek word *euangelion*, which had its origin in the custom of sending out heralds or messengers to towns and villages when a new monarch was crowned. The messengers announced the good news! One of the classic uses of the word dates back to 490 B.C., when a huge Persian army invaded Greece. A small Greek army from the city of Athens went out against the enemy. They met on the plains near a city called Marathon. The Athenians won. After the battle they picked one of their fastest runners, and instructed him to go home and tell the good news of the victory. The runner ran the whole distance, 26 miles, and shouted through the streets of Athens, "Rejoice, we have won!" and then he died from exhaustion. In the account in the Greek literature that tells the story, the runner is called an "evangelist." That story, by the way, explains why we call our long-distance race today a marathon. In modern Olympics, 385 yards have been added to the original 26 miles, but the name and the 26 miles originate with that story.

The word *evangelism* was made by changing the original Greek letters into English. One can see the similarity between the words *euangelion* and *evangelism*. In Greek the first two letters, *eu*, are a prefix that means "good." The root word, *angelos*, from which we get the word "angel," means "messenger." An evangelist is a good messenger, an evangel is a good message.

The New Testament, by the inspiration of the Holy Spirit, uses that word to refer to the coming of Jesus and the good news of His life, death, and resurrection. Gabriel said to Zechariah, "I was sent to . . . bring you this good news" (Luke 1:19). The angel told the shepherds on the plains of Bethlehem, "I bring you good news of a great joy" (Luke 2:10). The Greek New Testament describes how Jesus began his ministry: He came "evangelizing," "preaching Good News" (Mark 1:14). The same word, *euangelion*, is used throughout the book of Acts to describe the telling and preaching of the message of forgiveness and salvation in Jesus Christ.

A Witness Evangelizes

Today the word *evangelism* carries associations that are often full of emotions—sometimes negative ones. When some people hear the word they picture an emotional revival where people are pressured to come to the altar and make a confession for Christ. Or they see a well-intended evangelist confronting a person in a threatening manner with the words, "Are you saved, brother?" Sometimes people think that evangelism means Billy Graham or other radio and TV evangelists, itinerant preachers, or even Mormon young people who go door to door as, to use their term, "proselytizing missionaries." But the word evangelism has as its basic meaning the simple act of sharing the Good

19

News about Jesus Christ. So evangelism can be done by professionals in crusades, on radio and television, or in the pulpit. But it is also done by lay people witnessing to their neighbors and friends.

Many congregations have organized evangelism committees in order to help reach out to share the Gospel with the unchurched people of the community. To do this, lay people have been trained to make calls on the homes of the unchurched in order to present to them the Gospel in a formal way. These callers have often been called "evangelists." They are evangelizing, telling the Good News about Jesus Christ. An unfortunate distinction has sometimes developed through the use of the term "evangelist" in this way. Those who are trained with a method like Dialog Evangelism or Evangelism Explosion are thought of as the evangelists in the congregation. So it is concluded that they are the ones who evangelize!

But *every* Christian is a witness. A witness tells the Good News about Jesus Christ and thus is also evangelizing. Both the trained caller (called evangelist) and the person who witnesses spontaneously in daily life situations evangelize in that they both share the Gospel.

The term *evangelist* was first used for trained callers by those who developed and used Evangelism Explosion and Dialog Evangelism because the callers were thought to have been gifted by God for this special ministry. St. Paul in Eph. 4:11 speaks about the gifts God gave to the church: "His gifts were that some should be apostles, some prophets, some evangelists, some pastors and teachers." Philip, one of the seven deacons chosen by the early church (Acts 6) to assist the apostles was a man "full of the Spirit and of wisdom." Philip "evangelized" (*euangelizomai*) in Samaria, and many came to believe (Acts 8:12–13). Later Paul calls him "Philip the evangelist" (Acts 21:8). Whether the term "evangelist" is used today to refer to those called to travel from place to place to conduct crusades and special services, or to lay members who make calls in congregations, it needs to be remembered that every Christian evangelizes when he witnesses about Jesus Christ.

When Jesus said to His disciples, "you shall be my witnesses" (Acts 1:8), that is what He meant that they would do—tell others about Him and what He did to pay for the sins of the world by His death. They would tell that by His resurrection He gave eternal life to all. The disciples of Jesus Christ did that throughout history. Because the message of the Gospel came to us through their witness, you and I are disciples of Jesus Christ today. When infants are baptized, the message is conveyed by the Word in and with the water. The power is in the Word. Someone brought us to that Word. Someone told us. Now it is our turn to bring others to it.

A Disciple Witnesses with His Life

A disciple witnesses by telling others in words the Good News about Jesus Christ, but he also witnesses with his life. Jesus said to His disciples, "You are the salt of the earth. . . . You are the light of the world. . . . Let your light so shine before men, that they may see your good works and give glory to your Father who is in heaven" (Matt. 5:13–15). Again He said, "By this all men will know that you are My disciples, if you have love for one another" (John 13:35).

Living a committed Christian life does not convert people or explain what Jesus' death on the cross means. The good works of a Christian are the "consequence" of believing in Jesus and serve as the "bridge" over which the verbal explanation of the Gospel may enter the life of another person. A life of love can break down the barriers of prejudice and suspicion and open doors for a hearing of the Gospel. Thus a Christian life is the "partner" of the spoken Gospel message. It was a Lausanne Consultation on Evangelism and Social Responsibility in 1982[1] that used those words—*consequence, bridge,* and *partner.* Evangelism and social responsibility, the conference suggested, are like two blades of a pair of scissors or the two wings of a bird. This partnership is seen in the ministry of Jesus who not only preached the Gospel but fed the hungry and healed the sick. Proclamation and service went hand in hand. His words explained His works, and His works dramatized His words. Both were expressions of His compassion for people, and both should be ours.

My friend Lyle Muller suggests that he finds deeds that precede and follow his witness to be very helpful. But deeds without the spoken witness only point to oneself.

Irish monks evangelized much of Scotland, northern England, and parts of France, Switzerland, and Italy from the 6th to the 8th century. A group of 12 monks with a leader would leave their home monastery and go to a distant place to find seclusion, seeking to bring spiritual blessings to themselves. They would get permission from the ruler of the land, build crude shelters, and establish a routine of worship, work, and study. The people in the surrounding communities noticed the monks and how they lived. The monks' piety, self-denial, and charity was such a contrast to the savagery and immorality in which the people lived, that they wanted to learn how to be more like the monks. So the people asked the monks to instruct them. The monks, who had intended to enrich only their own lives, became missionaries who led others to Christ.[2]

To live as the "light" that reflects Jesus Christ, the "Light of the world," means that we are different from the people who live around us. Our Christian principles set us apart from the world. We look at things differently. We have different values. People caught up in the "world system" don't understand us. Richard Lischer in his book, *Speaking of Jesus*, suggests that a Christian risks ridicule and ostracism when he lives his Christian life and speaks of his Savior. The "authentic witness always finds himself slightly out of sync with society, articulating words no one wants to hear, engaging in acts of faithfulness no one understands."[3] He calls these the "little martyrdoms" of the Christian witness today.

A Disciple Witnesses with His Words

"We cannot but speak of what we have seen and heard," the apostles told the Sanhedrin (Acts 4:20). Not only would they be faithful to the new commandment to love as Christ loved (John 13:34), they would speak the message in words and explain its meaning. The Book of Acts, a testimony to the fact that God's Word accomplishes that which He purposes, records repeatedly that "the Word of God increased; and the number of the disciples multiplied" (Acts 6:7; cf. 12:24). Not only did the apostles "not cease teaching and preaching Jesus as the Christ" (Acts 5:42), but the early believers also witnessed to their faith. Luke notes that believers in the church at Jerusalem, scattered to other regions because of persecution, "went about preaching the word" (Acts 8:4).

Often the heathen world was impressed by the lives the early Christian disciples lived, and said, "how they love one another" or that they "turned the world upside down" (Acts 17:6). The disciples explained with words why they lived that way and urged others to believe as they did so they could experience the same hope of their future with God.

After his Pentecost sermon Peter was concerned that those who heard his message also believe it, and he pleaded, "Repent, and be baptized." And then, Scripture records, "he testified with many other words and exhorted them saying, 'Save yourselves' " (Acts 2:38–40).

A second-century public official reported to a Roman named Diognetus, "Christians cannot be distinguished from the rest of humanity by country or language or custom. They do not separate themselves into cities of their own . . . although they live in Greek and barbarian cities . . . and follow the usual customs of those cities, they *never cease to witness* to the reality of another city in which they live. . . ."[4]

The person. The Word. These two, the person and the Word, cannot be separated in Christian witness. Someone has compared the ingredients of a Christian witness to the three legs of an old-fashioned milking stool. The three legs on which a Christian witness rests are: What I am, What I do, and What I say. If one puts the words *am*, *do*, and *say* in this order: *say*, *am*, *do*, they can lead to the acronym SAD. And it is SAD when one of the three legs does not support the stool! Any of the three that fails leaves the Christian witness lopsided.

The people we admire the most are usually characterized by "congruence or genuineness," says Christian psychologist Kenneth Haugk. Who they say they are and what they do match up. "My guess is," he says, "the more you achieve congruence—distinctly Christian congruence—the more respect you will receive."[5] It is that kind of respect that opens the door for a hearing of the Gospel. If there is no such respect there may be rejection both of the behavior and the witness.

At the Mayor's Prayer Breakfast in St. Louis on Ash Wednesday 1984, the main speaker was the movie star Dean Jones who gave a testimony of his personal faith in Jesus Christ. He told how he had recently been offered a role as a middle-aged detective in a proposed TV series. After reading the script, he was pleased. It was well written and an interesting story. But there was one part where he, as a middle-aged detective, would go to bed with his female photographer. That he didn't like. So he met with the writer and producer and suggested ways to leave that out of the story. But they would not change, so he refused the job offer. He explained his decision to the 2,000 people at that breakfast. He had recently written to a 13-year-old girl who had asked for his advice as to what to do when her boy friend asked her to go to bed with him. He had tried in his letter to explain how a Christian deals with such issues. Then he said, "I could see that 13-year-old reading my letter and then watching me on the screen romping in bed and in a bathtub with someone who was not my wife. What a contradiction that would be!"

The walk and the talk must speak the same message or both will be rejected as not genuine or authentic. Disciples of Jesus Christ not only follow the teachings of Jesus Christ, but they try to be like Him, to be motivated by unselfish love, to show compassion for the needs and hurts of others, and to share with them the Way that brings life, "life in all its fullness" (John 10:10 TEV).

That is a Christian witness. It is not just witnessing by life, no matter how good that life is. It is not just witnessing with words, no matter how well they are said. It is not an "either-or" but a "both-and."

A pastor, serving in a run-down area of a large city, tells of visiting an elderly shut-in lady in a small apartment. She complained about her sore feet. When he examined them, he found open sores with maggots in them. Then he posed the question, "Should I tell her Jesus loves her or should I wash her dirty feet and clean her sores?" The answer is not "either-or" but "both-and." While he cares for her feet he can tell her about the care of a loving God—and he can do it in simple conversational terms without being "preachy."

Witnesses are disciples of Jesus Christ who share the Good News of the Gospel that they have come to know through the Scriptures and experienced in personal life. They share the message by both a life of love and words of Gospel. Our next chapter will discuss how witnesses deal with the fears of witnessing and show how to begin to witness.

For Further Study and Action

1. Read 2 Cor. 5:20 RSV and compare a "witness" with an "ambassador." In what ways do they do the same things? In what ways do they differ?
2. In 1 John 1:1–3, John speaks about proclaiming what "we have seen and heard." What senses were involved in the seeing and

hearing? To whom is he referring? What senses are involved in what we "see and hear" today?

3. In 2 Peter 1:16, Peter speaks about being "eyewitnesses." Check the cross references to Matt. 17:1–8; Mark 9:2–8, and Luke 9:28–36 for the event he refers to. How does this "seeing" give authenticity to his witness?

4. In what other ways could the evangelism callers from St. Matthew Lutheran Church, St. Louis, referred to in the opening story, have answered the question, "If God loves me, why would He let me live like this?"

5. If you are studying this book with a group, share an instance with the group when you witnessed with "word," with "life," and with both.

6. After reading this chapter you may feel guilty or depressed as you review the record of your personal witnessing. Read 1 Peter 1:18–23. You have been redeemed! You have been born again! You are growing up in your salvation!

7. Select one person whom you will make your "witness project" as you continue to read this book. Put this person on your prayer list and begin to develop a relationship, if you do not have one now, and try to find one way to share what Jesus means to you.

2. I for Intentional

Steve Cohen was giving the testimony of his conversion to a Sunday morning Bible class. He had been brought up in a Jewish home in Seattle and by the time he went to college he believed that it was important "to be a good person, to respect my fellow-man, and to remain loyal to Judaism." It was while he was in service, that Steve became aware of the difference between his life and that of his good friend, Alan. "I knew he had something in his life that I wanted in mine, but I didn't know what it was," Steve said.

Finally through the prayers and witness of his friend, Alan, and some rather strange experiences, Steve came to believe that Jesus Christ was the Messiah, his personal Savior and Lord. He told the Bible class that Sunday morning how Alan had prayed for him for two years and how Alan had witnessed to him by reading the Bible. Then he asked, "How do you witness to others?"

One well-intentioned lady got up and said, "Well, we don't do that in our church." That was hard for Steve to understand, and it is hard for me to understand. How can a Christian say "I don't witness?" Jesus said, "You shall be My witnesses" (Acts 1:8). When you and I bear the name of Christ and claim to belong to a Christian church, everything we do or say is a witness to our genuineness as to what it means to be a Christian and a member of the Christian church. It is either a positive or a negative witness, but it is a witness. What the lady really meant is that she did not talk to other people about her faith, invite them to believe, invite them to her church, or give them religious literature from her church.

In the first chapter we discussed the meaning of witness. In this chapter we will deal with the desire to witness. Even though we understand what a witness is and have some thoughts on how to do it, we will not do it without a motive, a desire to do it. And even if we have a desire to do it, there are often barriers that are too great for our desire to overcome. We will first examine some of those barriers and then suggest ways to begin to take the initiative in witnessing.

There are many ways to outline the various kinds of barriers that hinder our witnessing. Irv Rasmussen, director of the Lutheran Evangelism Association, speaks in his training lectures about the obstacles: The devil, the world, and me. The devil will do anything to prevent a witness to the Gospel. The world doesn't want to hear it. And there are obstacles or barriers within me that prevent me from witnessing. We will summarize some of the things that prevent me from witnessing under these barriers:

Barrier 1: What I Believe
Barrier 2: What I Fear
Barrier 3: What I Am Unable to Do

Barrier 1: What I Believe

In the book, *Study of Generations*,[1] which examined the beliefs and practices of the Lutherans in the United States, it is reported that individuals surveyed responded to this statement: "God is satisfied if I live the best life I can." Seventy percent of those surveyed agreed with that statement. Do you? Think a moment. If God is satisfied with my best, how can Jesus claim to be "the way, the truth, and the life"? How can He say, "No one comes to the Father, but by Me" (John 14:6)? If all I need to do is live the best life I can, I have no need of Jesus Christ. If God is satisfied with the best I can do, Jesus came for nothing.

That attitude fits in with the American philosophy of "live and let live." We believe in allowing people to be what they want to be and to believe what they want to believe. We call it "tolerance," and we say we must accept the fact that we live in a pluralistic society of many different faiths and beliefs. My neighbor can be a good neighbor by trying to live the best life he can. Is he then right with God? If he is, then I don't have to witness to him about Jesus Christ. My friend can be a good Rotarian or Lion and demonstrate how good he is by the unselfish service he does and the contributions he makes. I don't have to witness to him about Jesus Christ because he is trying to live the best he can.

Closely related to this belief that "God is satisfied if I live the best life I can" is another statement from *Study of Generations* that reads: "I should not try to change another person's belief." Forty percent agreed with that statement.[2]

What I believe, then, about how a person makes peace with God and about my responsibility to tell him about the way to do it becomes a barrier to witnessing. How do I deal with this subtle desire to be tolerant, nonjudgmental, accepting, and yet take a stand for the unique place of faith in Jesus Christ as the only way to be right with God? I must first review what is involved if I believe the message of Scripture, "There is no other name under heaven given among men by which we must be saved," as Peter said (Acts 4:12). "The wages of sin is death, but the free gift of God is eternal life in Christ Jesus our Lord" (Rom. 6:23).

Those passages tell me that my neighbor, my fellow Rotarian, or my own relative—no matter how good a person he is—is a sinner. Anyone who lives without the forgiveness and the grace of God will go to hell. All have sinned and need to know Jesus Christ as their personal Savior. How are these "good" people going to know their condition? How are they going to have the opportunity to come to faith? If I am the person who is in a position to talk to one of them, perhaps God has put me there to be the person to speak.

But now come the excuses. "It won't do any good. He is satisfied and content with his life. My witness won't make him believe. I don't know what to say. I don't want to offend him." Again, I must examine what I believe so that what I believe is not a barrier but a means to create the desire to witness. Do I really believe the promises of the power of the Gospel? God promised through His great Old Testament evangelist, Isaiah, "My word . . . shall not return to Me empty, but it shall accomplish that which I purpose, and prosper in the thing for which I sent it" (Is. 55:11). St. Paul said, "The gospel . . . is the power of God for salvation" (Rom. 1:16).

At a meeting of the Religious Broadcasters, the former aid to President Nixon, Charles Colson, who went to prison for his involvement in the Watergate cover-up, and Eldridge Cleaver, the former leader of the Black Panthers, sat on a panel together in one of the sectional meetings. Both men had come to faith in Jesus Christ. They told what that meant in their lives, after which there was a discussion period. During the discussion, Chuck Colson answered a question this way: "Yes, Eldridge and I were once bitter enemies. But we both had one thing in common, we wanted to change society. I thought you changed society through political power, so I climbed the ladder and got next to the highest power in the country, the President. Eldridge believed you changed society through violence, and he went to the street. But today we have both learned that the only way people are really changed is through the power of Jesus Christ."

Yet another aspect of the barrier is that my life contradicts what I say that I believe. In one survey, respondents were asked why Christians don't witness more. The top answer was "sin." Christians hesitate to witness to people who see how they live because they are afraid of the response, "practice what you preach." Our witness is enhanced or hindered by the life that accompanies the witness.

Someone has compared the witness that is dulled with an inconsistent Christian life to church bells being "iced." Clear, well-cast church bells can give a dull, muted sound in January when snow and ice accumulates on them. So a Christian's clear, ringing testimony to faith in Jesus Christ can be "iced-up" by pride, jealousy, materialism, hatred, lying, gossip, envy, and other vices that characterize the "old nature." When my neighbor sees me fighting with my wife, he may not hear my witness. The friend who sees me regularly sitting in a bar, imbibing a little too much once in a while, may not be ready to go to church with me on Sunday. Not only can my life "ice-up" my witness, but it may also prevent me from giving it because I am ashamed of the way I am living.

How do I deal with this barrier? Examine what the Bible says about sin. "If we confess our sins, He is faithful and just, and will forgive our sins and cleanse us from all unrighteousness" (1 John 1:9). God forgives because of Christ. The sinful nature is still there. My "flesh" and "spirit" struggle continually. I will never be perfect this side of heaven (Gal. 5:17). In fact, I must say with St. Paul, "I do not do the good I want, but the evil I do not want is what I do" (Rom. 7:19). That does not excuse a sinful life. By the power of the Spirit within me I seek to overcome sinful habits, and the fruit of the Spirit grows in my life (Gal. 5:22). As long as I live the new life in Christ, I can witness to my neighbor, even though I am not perfect.

I don't witness to my neighbor by pointing to my life. I point to Jesus Christ and tell my neighbor that in Jesus Christ I have forgiveness of my sins and through Jesus Christ I am dealing with my weak, sinful, selfish nature. In fact that is what is so wonderful about God! Because of Christ, God in His love receives a sinner like me, forgives me and changes me. What "amazing grace!"

Barrier 2: What I Fear

Every time I ask people at a workshop to list the top three reasons why they don't witness more, I can be sure that one of those reasons will be "fear." The fears are listed in different ways: Fear of being rejected, fear of not knowing what to say, fear of getting too personal, fear of ridicule, and so on. In a study of witnessing and nonwitnessing members of the Southern Baptist Conference the three top hindrances to witnessing given by both the witnessing and the nonwitnessing group put the fears in different language:

1. Lack of dependence on the Holy Spirit
2. Lack of knowledge about witnessing
3. Personality is not the type to do witnessing

A Southern Baptist Seminary professor of evangelism, Delos Miles, wrote a book titled *Overcoming Barriers to Witnessing.*[3] He lists barriers, with excuses that are given for each barrier. Most of the points he covers are included, at least in a small way, in our three barriers, "What I Believe," "What I Fear" and "What I Am Unable to Do." As you read Miles's list, check yourself to see if you ever make any of the same or similar excuses:

1. The Fear Barrier—"I'm afraid."
2. The Perfection Barrier—"I'm not good enough."
3. The Spiritual Gift Barrier—"I don't have the gift."
4. The Professional Barrier—"That's a minister's work."
5. The Model Barrier—"I'm no Billy Graham."
6. The Time Barrier—"I don't have the time."
7. The Knowledge Barrier—"I don't know how."
8. The Power Barrier—"I don't have the power to do that."
9. The Theological Barrier—"I don't believe."
10. The Stranger Barrier—"You can't witness to total strangers."
11. The Age Barrier—"I'm too old."
12. The Kinship-Friendship Barrier—"I'm too close."

Some of the above excuses are just that—excuses because a person does not have the desire to witness. But some of the excuses are based on facts. In some denominations the history and tradition has been that the minister did most of the witnessing. Lay members did not talk in Bible classes or church meetings about their personal relationship to Jesus Christ. They did not develop the habit of inviting other people to their church, let alone tell them about their faith. The cultures out of which some of these denominations came were so formal that one seldom expressed emotion or personal conviction. It was proper and acceptable to say, "I make it a rule never to discuss religion or politics." A person from that kind of cultural upbringing finds it hard to change.

Paul Foust in the book, *Reach Out: Evangelism for the Joy of It,* describes how Satan uses the "Fear Complex" to "block the flow of the Gospel." Foust says, "Fear always has been and always will be a problem for every Christian . . . Fear is the most common paralyzing obstacle to Christian witness."[4]

When our Lord Jesus was being tried the night before His crucifixion, a servant girl said to Peter, "Are not you also one of His disciples?" Big, strong, boastful Simon Peter had a chance to witness, but he wilted and flew into a rage as he denied his Lord three times. Foust uses this example. Place a 12-foot plank on the ground and ask a group of people to walk on it from one end to the other. They will have no problem. Suspend the same plank 50 feet in the air, from a ladder at each end, and then ask the same people to walk across it. Probably none of them can. They are frozen by fear.[5]

How do I begin to deal with the barrier of fear? Lets take two specific fears that are commonly verbalized, "I am afraid of being rejected," and "I am afraid I won't know what to say." Why am I afraid of "being rejected or ridiculed?" Is it because I want to be accepted and loved by people and I need that kind of support from others? That may be a very real psychological need, but I find help in knowing that I am always accepted by God, that He is with me in my every effort to witness, "Lo, I am with you always" (Matt. 28:20). Rejection or ridicule are hard to accept, but I need to expect it. Jesus said, "If the world hates you, know that it has hated Me before it hated you" (John 15:18). Lischer, in *Speaking of Jesus,* warns of the "little martyrdoms" that every Christian must expect. We Christians will always seem a little out of sync with the world. We live a life-style based on different values and standards. We speak of a God many do not want to hear about.[6]

The story is told of a mother who had aspirations for her son's future as a pianist. She took her little boy to a concert of

Paderewski, the great Polish pianist. They arrived early and sat very near the front. While speaking with those sitting next to her, she did not notice that her boy left his seat. When the lights dimmed she almost panicked when she saw he was gone. Looking up just as Paderewski was walking on the stage, she saw her boy sitting at the big grand piano in the center of the stage. Frantically she climbed out of her seat and was about to rush up on the stage to retrieve him, when the great pianist motioned her to stay away. He walked up to the boy and encouraged him to continue to play. He was playing "Twinkle, Twinkle, Little Star" with one finger. Paderewski stood behind the piano bench and with his left hand reached around the boy and began adding notes to the tune, and then put his right hand on the keyboard as well to embellish the simple melody. When they finished, the audience broke into a joyful applause for a beautiful piece of music.

Christian witnessing works in a similar way. I speak my "Twinkle, Twinkle," but through me God speaks His Word. Jesus warned His disciples that they would be persecuted when they witnessed, but He added, "Do not be anxious how you are to speak or what you are to say; for what you are to say will be given to you in that hour; for it is not you who speak, but the Spirit of your Father speaking through you" (Matt. 10:19–20).

Barrier 3: What I Am Unable to Do

Much has been said in the church in recent years about the New Testament spiritual gifts, and dozens of books and studies have been printed. St. Paul explained to the Romans that all Christians, although members of the one church, nevertheless have different functions. Paul tells these believers that all of us "have . . . gifts that differ according to the grace given to us" (Rom. 12:4–6). He calls the church the body of Christ as he proclaims to Christians in Corinth, "To each is given the manifestation of the Spirit for the common good" (1 Cor. 12:7). Peter writes, "As each has received a gift, employ it for one another, as good stewards of God's varied grace" (1 Peter 4:10).

This emphasis on the spiritual gifts can remove a burden of guilt and free Christians to explore and use the gifts that God has given them to use as they "function" in the body. But unfortunately it has also allowed some Christians to use the excuse, "I don't have the gift of evangelist." That may be true and may be a reason for some people not to be involved in the ongoing calling program of the congregation (see the discussion in chapter 1 on the gift of evangelist), but it is *not* a legitimate excuse for not witnessing! Jesus calls every Christian to witness. As each Christian uses the gifts God gives, that activity becomes a witness. This is the witness of life to which can be added the witness of lip.

C. Peter Wagner in his lectures on spiritual gifts often uses the illustration of a lady who was moved by her pastor's sermon on the need for every member to be a functioning part of the body, for everyone to do something in the church. After the service she said to the pastor, "But there isn't anything I can do." The pastor thought about it for a while and later that day he called her on the telephone. "A family by the name of Black has moved in down the street from you. Why don't you bake your best apple strudel and take it over to them as a welcome. That is something you can do." She was delighted. The pastor repeated his request a number of times and pretty soon she became known in the congregation for her welcome to newcomers. And pretty soon, when people asked her why she brought them an apple strudel, she could say "This is a way I can show my love for God . . . and for you." She made a simple witness.

She did not have the gift of being an evangelist, but she had a gift of helping or serving and, as she used that gift, she learned to witness. Some Christians do have a difficult time articulating their faith—perhaps partly because of a home environment in which they did not talk about God and their relationship with Him. Or perhaps partly because they have never talked about Him even in their church meetings. But by God's grace we can deal with this barrier too. We can learn. We can grow in our ability and skill to verbalize what we believe and to share it with another person. We learn by doing, finding ways in our association with other Christians to practice talking about our faith, in our home, our Bible class, and in special witness training seminars or classes. Then, beginning where we are, we learn how to speak to others when the opportunity arises.

Take the Initiative

As we begin to deal with the barriers that prevent us from witnessing, God's Spirit develops in us the desire to share our faith with others. Then, as we have the opportunity, we can learn to take the initiative. In fact, that is about the only way to develop skills in witnessing and to discover the method that works best for us personally. In the kind of secular society in which we live, conversation about God and religious things does not often "just happen."

Sometimes the person we are talking with may even want to discuss a religious question or concern but waits for us to say the first word. Our own human nature urges us to wait for the other person to indicate a readiness to talk about religion, or we rationalize that this is not the right time. A better opportunity will come at another time.

It takes a conscious effort to make a transition to talk about spiritual things. One way to do that is to seek to move the conversation to church background or participation and then on to a witness of faith. Let me illustrate. I went to my barber a few days after a big snow storm. As we talked I asked, "Did you make it in those two days?" He replied, "I closed the first day and came in a while the second day but there wasn't much business. If I miss a day, the next day is a little busier and I make up part of the business, but if I miss two days, I never make it up."

"That's the way it is in church, too, at least at our church," I continued and told him a little about my church and then led into the question, "Is it like that at your church?" He told me a little about his church, remarking especially about how people gave at his church. That allowed me to move into my testimony!

"I give a percentage of my income, so once a month I write a check for each Sunday of the month. Then if I miss one Sunday I take it the next Sunday, since the check is already written."

He carried the conversation further. "The church isn't the same today. We are losing our young people because we are not teaching them the same as what I was taught. I learned when I was young that when you sinned you go to hell. Today all they teach is love and forgiveness.

That gave me an opening to move from "church talk" to "faith talk" and especially about what the Bible says about forgiveness. I used the same method once again—I asked questions:

"What do you believe about forgiveness?"

"Does God forgive all our sins?"

"How do we receive that forgiveness?"

I questioned. I listened. And then, as the opportunity came, I gave a personal testimony. I had intended to witness as I began the conversation, and so I consciously directed the conversation, using this method: *Question-Listen-Tell*. So the conversation moved: *chitchat-church-faith*.

That method works best for me right now. Each person must find the one that works best for them. Delos Miles[7] has developed what he calls the FORM anagram: He starts the conversation by talking about the family, moves to occupation and personal interest, and then on to religion and his Gospel message. So his anagram looks like this:

> F — Family
> O — Occupation, interests
> R — Religion
> M — Message

In the next chapter we will expand on the "Question-Listen-Tell" method. And we'll share the "three-story" way of talking about faith. But before that we want to discuss the use of witnessing helps.

Learn to Use Helps

I may want to witness. I may be dealing with my barriers. And I may intend to take the initiative in conversation. Even so, many opportunities may still slip by me because I do not take that opportunity. One way I find helpful is to use "conversation starters." They work most often in casual contacts with people. They open the door so I can give a simple witness or leave a printed message with the person. Conversation starters may be personal items that I wear on my clothing or they may be pictures, plaques, or mottoes that I use in my home, office, or car.

For a number of years I wore a "Jesus" pin[8] on the lapel of my suit. It's a white pin with the word *Jesus* printed on it in reverse computer type, which makes it hard to read. In fact, I have discovered that while children and young people can read the pin (or a card with the same word on it), people 40 and over have difficulty seeing the word "Jesus" at first glance. So, people see the prominent pin on my lapel and ask, "What is that? What does that say?" Some have even asked, "Are those tire tracks? Is that Hebrew? What company do you work for?" I usually respond, "It says the same thing as my card," and hand them the card with the same word. The card has a message with Bible verses about Jesus on the back. I help them read the word from the card, and then we talk about Jesus. It's almost automatic.

As I checked out of a Holiday Inn in Omaha one morning, a

middle-aged lady behind the desk asked, "What does your pin say?" I went through the usual procedure and gave her the card. She began by reading out loud the small type below the word Jesus, "The above word can change your life." Just then a young lady also behind the counter came over, glanced at the card and said, "Why that says *Jesus*. Can't you see it?" The first lady just looked at me. Then she said, "I guess He could change my life . . . if I would let Him. Can I keep the card?"

"Certainly," I replied, "if you promise to read the passages on the back." With that I had to leave, for other customers were waiting to check out.

Other conversation starters include:

> Pins with mottoes like "Try Jesus"
> Fishhook or fish pins
> Simon Peter pins (shepherd staff with fish hook across to make a cross)
> Crosses as pins or jewelry
> Butterfly or other symbols

There are many others. The point is that often a simple thing like a pin or piece of jewelry can start a conversation that leads to a Christian witness. Some people may think of them as gimmicks, but without them the conversation often does not take place. The question that starts the witness is in the mind of the person who sees the pin. That person starts the conversation. You do not force a witness.

There are other kinds of helps in addition to conversation starters. There are helps to communicate the message of the Gospel, such as tracts that can be left with a person and witnessing booklets[9] that can be used to present a message. Some booklets are written to be used that way. You give the person with whom you are speaking a copy and you go through it page by page in a "presentation of the Gospel" and then leave the booklet with the person. This is especially helpful, of course, when a witness finds it hard to explain the way of salvation when the opportunity arises.

Some people witness through the distribution of tracts. Tracts can be given in person, left where people will pick them up, or sent in the mail. There are hundreds of different tracts available from various sources, such as the American Tract Society; Concordia Tract Mission; Faith, Prayer, and Tract League;

and Good News Publishers.[10] A folder entitled "10 Tips for Tract Users"[11] suggests:

1. *Never distribute tracts without praying.* Ask the Holy Spirit to bless the reader.
2. *Give tracts which are appropriate.* Simple Gospel tracts will fit general needs for every person but use tracts which address specific needs when possible.
3. *Talk with your subject if possible.* This helps to know the person's needs. Conversation can stimulate interest in reading the tract and point to a thought or Bible verse in the tract.
4. *Always offer tracts with a smile.*
5. *Don't force tracts upon people.*
6. *Use attractive tracts.*
7. *Keep tracts in good condition.*
8. *Use positive, constructive tracts.*
9. *Think up new ways to use tracts.* Place tracts in letters, greeting cards. Place them where people are likely to pick them up and read them.
10. *Begin with one tract every day.*

Some people prefer to use the Scripture itself to help them speak the Gospel message. A New Testament can be marked so that a theme is written in the margin beside one passage that is underlined. The next reference (or page number) is written in at the bottom of the page with the words "Turn to . . . ." This way, one can move through the Bible from sin, to punishment for sin, to the death of Jesus Christ for sin, to forgiveness, to faith, to growing in faith. (See the method suggested in the Study and Action section at the end of this chapter.)

So many helps are available to get us started as we seek to witness about our faith in Jesus Christ. The helps can be a good beginning, a starting place for the witness to continue to learn how to speak about Jesus Christ. The important thing is that we begin to witness—intentionally. We can do that as we deal with the barriers that prevent us from witnessing and as we let the Spirit of God continue to develop the desire to witness in our hearts.

One of the helpful ways to speak the Gospel message that seldom creates resentment is to speak from a personal point of view. This approach helps to build trust and personal relationship. We tell what we have "seen and heard" about Jesus in the Scripture and in our relationship with Him. We often call this our "Testimony." That's what the next chapter is about.

For Further Study and Action

1. Someone has said that the most frequently uttered prayer is, "God damn it/you." What does it mean that God damns someone? Why would He do that? How does this relate to our witness? Read these passages:
   Mark 16:16 _____
   Matt. 23:33 _____
   Matt. 25:41 _____

2. Read the passages noted below. Why did Jesus have compassion? Are we concerned about friends or relatives who are not disciples of Jesus Christ?
   Matt. 9:36 _____
   Luke 13:34 _____

3. Satan often seems to be in control of our world and of us. But there is a power that can deal with Satan. Read Luke 4:1–13. How can we handle the barriers to witnessing that Satan uses against us? Read also Rom. 1:16 and Acts 1:8.

4. When Jesus told us to "make disciples" He also promised that He would be with us always (Matt. 28:19–20). Read the following promises of what the Holy Spirit will do. Jot down behind each passage what the Spirit will do:
   John 14:13–14 _____
   John 14:26 _____
   John 15:26–27 _____
   John 16:12–15 _____

5. Try experimenting with "conversation starters," a simple attractive cross, a pin, or some piece of jewelry. When people look at it, take the initiative, if they don't, and say, "Oh, do you like my . . ." or "Did you notice my . . ." or 'I'm glad you noticed my . . . . It gives me a chance to tell you what it means to me."

6. Continue to pray for the one person you selected as you read chapter 1. Select a tract to give that person, try your "conversation starter" with that person, or share your marked New Testament.

7. Try marking a New Testament to use to witness to another person or to give to someone. Follow the directions below, underlining or highlighting the passages indicated and printing

neatly, in the margin at the top of the page and the bottom of the page, the words indicated.

Print on the inside cover: "This is a marked New Testament. God loves you and will give you eternal life. See 1 John 3:1, page _____."

Top of Page	*Mark the Verse*	*Bottom of the Page*
p. _____ God loves you	John 3:16	But man rejects God's love. See p.
p. _____ Sin separates man from God	Rom. 3:23	The result is tragic. See p. _____
p. _____ The penalty is spiritual death	Rom. 6:23	Christ took our place. See p. _____
p. _____ Christ paid for our sin	2 Cor. 5:21	Christ is the only way. See p. _____
p. _____ Jesus is the way to life with God	John 14:6	Only believe! See p. _____
p. _____ Receive Him, believe Him	John 1:12	You can have life in its fullness. See p. _____
p. _____ Jesus makes life meaningful	John 10:10b	The Holy Spirit makes you a witness. See p. _____
p. _____ The Holy Spirit makes you a witness	Acts 1:8	

3. T for Testimony

While serving in the Marine Corps, I went with a friend to a Protestant service conducted by a Baptist chaplain. As we walked into the chapel, he said to me, "Do you want to give your testimony today?" I had come directly from the seminary into the military service and had lived a relatively sheltered life in Lutheran schools all the way from grade one through the first two years at the seminary, when I dropped out. I had very little association with other denominations. I just didn't know what he meant when he said, "Do you want to give your testimony?" What was a "testimony"? How do you give a testimony? I politely declined—and then listened carefully to those who did give a testimony in the service.

I discovered that a testimony is telling one's personal religious experiences or a statement of what one believes. It often includes an account of one's life before conversion, how one came to faith in Christ, and then the difference Christ has made. Just as we count the years by using B.C. (Before Christ) and A.D. (Anno Domini, in the year of the Lord; after Christ), so a testimony is usually thought of in most Christian circles as telling what life was like before and after Christ came into that life or into a particular problem in life.

Testimony Is Telling

While Lutherans usually do not have lay members of the congregation give such personal testimonies in our services, this kind of testimony can take place in more informal gatherings in the church and especially in personal witnessing. St. Paul often used his testimony to witness. One example of this is in Acts 22. Paul had been arrested in Jerusalem and after getting permission from the tribune to speak to the crowd, he began to tell his personal story. He started, "I am a Jew, born at Tarsus in Cilicia, but brought up in this city at the feet of Gamaliel." He went on to tell about the time before he came to know and believe that

40

Jesus of Nazareth was the Messiah. "I persecuted this Way to the death, binding and delivering to prison both men and women."

Then Paul told about his conversion: "I fell to the ground and heard a voice saying to me, 'Saul, Saul, why do you persecute Me?' And I answered . . ."

Finally, the apostle told how he was baptized and called to be God's witness to the Gentiles. That was his testimony!

In the Old Testament the word for "testimony" is often used as a synonym for the "law" or "the commandments of God." The New Testament word often translated "testimony" is the Greek word *martureo*, the same word that in other places is translated "witness." When Jesus debated with the Pharisees about what He was teaching, He said, "Even if I do bear witness to Myself, My testimony is true" (John 8:14). When Jesus told the disciples that they would be arrested and persecuted, He told them that the purpose was "to bear testimony before them" (Matt. 10:18). In each of these cases and many others in Scripture, the same Greek word *martureo* appears. It may be variously translated, e.g., "witness" and "testify."In the acrostic that forms the outline of this *Witness Primer*, I use the word *testimony* to mean the same thing as *witness*—a telling of what "I have seen and heard." My testimony includes what I have learned about Jesus Christ from the Scripture and what this means in my life.

The last chapter suggested a method of beginning an intentional witness: The Q-L-T (Question-Listen-Tell) method. I use it to start the conversation. As I do so, I try to move the content of the discussion from C to C to F (chitchat-church-faith). As we think about T for Testimony we will discuss ways to tell about our faith. To do that, we think about three stories.

I Tell My Story

Many writers in recent years have used the concept of teaching people how to witness by using the "Three-Story Method." The exact details may differ slightly. I will use the three story idea in a little different way. My way is not copied from any specific author and may even vary somewhat from some of the authors. I am using it in the way that I have found helpful in my own witness and others say that they have found it helpful too, as I have discussed it in Witness Workshops.

The three stories are: *My Story*, *Your Story* and *His Story*. I am open to telling *My Story* and ready to listen to *Your Story*.

At the same time, I try to relate both of our stories to *His Story*, or as some people suggest, God's Story. As one uses this concept, several dangers are to be avoided. First, one must be careful not to press too strongly on Your Story and ask questions in such a way that the other person feels that this is a cross-examination or prying into personal affairs. One must be sensitive, watch the body language, and catch the signals that tell when a person becomes uncomfortable or irritated. To avoid this, there must be a proper mixture of asking, listening, and telling.

The second danger is that, in telling My Story, I overemphasize myself and underemphasize Jesus Christ. This often happens when celebrities tell of dramatic conversions from the drug or alcohol scene to the Christian faith. The hearer is impressed about all the terrible things the person did, but doesn't remember much about who Jesus Christ is and what He has done. In my witnessing conversation I need to keep a balance and remember my goal: I want to share the Good News about Jesus Christ, so that the person to whom I am talking can believe and become a disciple of Jesus Christ. I use the personal pronoun "I" only in order to accomplish that goal! I must weave the two together— the objective story of the life, death, and resurrection of Jesus Christ as I have come to know it from Scripture, and what this means to me in my life. I use the "I" in order to help build a trust relationship with the person to whom I am speaking and to encourage that person to become personal also and speak about his or her faith. Here is an example:

A paper salesman, who comes to my office occasionally, invited me to lunch one day. I assumed that this free lunch was for the purpose of presenting his latest sales offer. But at lunch I discovered that my friend didn't want to talk about business at all—he wanted to talk about religion. He was a Reform Jew and we had already talked previously in the office about Christianity and Judaism. Now he wanted some privacy and more time to talk. The big question he had on his mind was, "What is the real difference between my faith and yours?" He asked questions like: "I believe in God; you believe in Jesus. What's the difference?" Or, "I believe that God forgives my sins; you believe that Jesus forgives your sins. What's the difference?" I had difficulty answering his questions on an intellectual, rational basis. My arguments didn't mean much to him. I tried asking questions and listening to his real concerns, but my telling didn't work.

Finally my salesman friend asked, "You believe that Jesus will take you to heaven, and I believe that God will take me to heaven. What's the difference?" It finally dawned on me that he wanted to hear why I personally believed in Jesus Christ. So I started to use "I" and tell more of "My Story." I believe the Spirit led. "The difference as I see it is that I am not good enough to go to heaven. God is holy, and I am a sinner. He will not take me to heaven unless something is done with my sins. That's why I believe in Jesus. Jesus died on the cross to pay for my sins, and when I look at the cross I know that my sins are paid for. Because of that cross I believe that God forgives me. So I am sure of my forgiveness and of my place in heaven."

My friend looked at me in a strange way and said, "I never heard anything like that before, that someone would have to take care of my sins." Then I could show him that the prophet Isaiah had said the same thing: "He was wounded for our transgressions, He was bruised for our iniquities; upon Him was the chastisement that made us whole, and with His stripes we are healed" (Is. 53:5). My Bible and his Bible agreed: "For our sake He made Him to be sin who knew no sin, so that in Him we might become the righteousness of God" (2 Cor. 5:21).

As I witnessed, I combined my personal testimony and the objective statements of the Scripture. It is certainly possible for personal experience to focus more on human feelings than on Christ. That can lead to a kind of subjectivism that replaces the objective Gospel. But because that might possibly happen, we should not automatically conclude that all personal testimony is subjective! Our witness can be both objective and personal at the same time. The apostolic witness included very objective facts, and yet some very personal experiences too.

The records of the life, death, and resurrection of Jesus Christ by the four evangelists are not identical. Each writer had "seen and heard" the same things. But their accounts are different, because the Holy Spirit used different individuals and different personalities to address different audiences.

In a similar way, we who have become disciples of Jesus Christ differ from each other. The Gospel has met different personal needs, so our testimonies are somewhat different. When we share our testimony with others, the testimonies are different, because God deals with us as individuals. Yet there is a basic objective witness that is the same, because it is based on the factual history of who Jesus is and what He has done for us as recorded in the Scriptures. The goal never changes: to present Jesus Christ as Savior and Lord in order that others may become His disciples.

When I was teaching a class on Christian Witness at Concordia Teachers College, Seward, Nebraska, I always gave this assignment: "Write a statement of at least 300 words entitled, 'What Jesus Means to Me.' " As I made the assignment, I would say, "I will not ask you to do something that I will not do." Then I would proceed to give my personal testimony about what Jesus meant in my life. One year after making that testimony, a student came to me to say, "I have never heard anything like a personal testimony. I grew up in a Christian home and went to Christian day school and Sunday school all my life, but I have never heard a teacher talk about what his personal faith in Jesus meant for his daily life. Thanks, it helped me apply my faith to my life."

Yes, there is danger of becoming "subjective" and making more of the "I" than of Jesus, but great blessing can come through personal testimony. It helps to communicate and apply the objective Gospel of Jesus Christ.

We must not be like the so-called Christian who said, "My faith means so much to me that I never talk about it." The important thing here is that whether we are accustomed to the more objective witness or the more personal witness, we can learn to combine them both through study and conscious effort and practice. We can develop a witness that is truly objective and yet very personal.

Examples from Scripture

The Scriptures provide many examples of witnessing that are both objective and subjective. Scripture clearly teaches an "objective justification" for all sinners by the death of Jesus Christ on the cross. At the same time, the Bible teaches that each person must come to faith individually and thus be justified. Theologians call this "subjective justification."

Psalm 23 points to the objective truth of a God who provides for all our needs, but it is spoken by one who knew Him personally and who spoke in very subjective language:

"The Lord is *my* shepherd, *I* shall not want; He makes *me* lie down in green pastures. . . . He restores *my* soul. . . . *I* shall dwell in the house of the Lord forever."

44

The demoniac out of whom Jesus cast the legion of devils was told by Jesus, "Go home to your friends, and tell them how much the Lord has done for you, and how He has had mercy on you" (Mark 5:19).

The Samaritans at Sychar first believed "because of the woman's testimony." That testimony was a personal witness of her experience with Christ: "He told me all that I ever did" (John 4:39).

St. Paul's Epistles are full of personal testimony: "Christ . . . lives in me" (Gal. 2:20). "For me to live is Christ, and to die is gain" (Phil. 1:21–24). "I do not understand my own actions. For I do not do what I want, but I do the very thing I hate. . . . Wretched man that I am!" But then Paul points the way by showing how he personally found help. "Thanks be to God through Jesus Christ our Lord!" (Rom. 7:15–25).

The Good News about Jesus Christ is usually communicated more convincingly when the witness's personal experience of it points to the objective truth of the Gospel, "the power of God for salvation" (Rom. 1:16). When one seeks to witness by presenting the objective statements of Scripture without the personal context, it often comes across as an impersonal statement, as giving the message that "I am better than you are," as judgmental and condemnatory, and so may be rejected without receiving a hearing.

Flying home from a conference, I read an article on EST (Erhard Seminars Training) from an airline magazine. The man sitting next to me saw the large print of the article and asked, "What do you think of that?"

"Oh, it sounds like some kind of brainwashing system to me," I replied.

"Oh, no," he insisted, "it really works."

"What works?" I asked, starting my Q-L-T (Question-Listen-Tell). Then I listened, asking a few questions as he told me his story. He was a middle-aged businessman returning home to Belleville, Illinois. Some months before, a close friend of his, a man about the same age, had died suddenly of a heart attack. "That got to me," he said. "I knew that I could go the same way, especially if I didn't do something about the tension in my life— my hectic pace and the competition of the business world. I went to TM (Transcendental Meditation). Now for 15 minutes every morning and evening I meditate. Now I get along fine."

"But what about your religion?" I inquired. He had told me that he was a member of the United Church of Christ.

"That doesn't do anything for my tension."

Now was a good time for my personal testimony—"My Story." I knew that in TM one recites a mantra (a mystical word or phrase) over and over again as one sits motionless for 15 minutes. "I don't see how saying such a phrase could help me, unless it would be like self-hypnosis. I deal with my tension by listening to God speak to me in His Word, and I talk to Him in prayer. Every morning I read my Bible and spend time meditating on what it means, what it is saying to me. Then I talk to God about that message and about my problems and tensions and ask Him for His help that day. In Jesus Christ I have forgiveness of all my sins and failures, and that gives me peace and contentment."

I had listened to *his story*. I had told *my story* in a way that connected our need for dealing with tension to *His Story*—the Good News about Jesus.

I Listen to Your Story

In order to use the three-story method I need to be open and willing to take the risk of telling my own story. But I must also be ready to listen. And this is a problem for many people. We can think about 500 words a minute but we can only speak about 125 words. So as we listen, we have extra "thinking time." We tend to use that extra time to think ahead and plan what we will say in response. We judge ahead of time, before we hear what the other person says. Sometimes we even let our minds wander to a different subject entirely. But each one of us can learn to listen better—if we want to learn. The desire to learn how to listen and to practice repeating what is said, is often called "active listening." It grows out of a caring concern for the other person—a genuine desire to help and to communicate a Gospel message of hope and joy.

Dr. Thomas Gordon of Effectiveness Training, Inc., lists four ways we can become better listeners:

1. Passive listening (silence)
2. Acknowledgment responses (body movement or "uh-huh," "Oh?", "I see," "Go on.")
3. Door Openers (open-ended questions, e.g., "Do you want to talk about it?")

4. Active listening (paraphrasing; asking questions to check content and feelings)

Martin Lundi, in the *Witness Workshop Manual*, combines some of Gordon's emphasis on listening and uses the term "Effective Listening."[1] Lundi suggests that through this kind of listening we can create open doors and opportunities for witness. In every conversation there is:

1. A meaning, a message, or a concern.
2. A code, the method by which a person seeks to communicate his message. This may be direct or indirect, depending on the person's openness and the relationship he has with the person to whom he is talking.
3. An interpretation. I interpret the code to discover the meaning or message. This is a guess, but it can be checked out by dialog.

Here is an example that Lundi gives:

The Situation: A fellow worker, Andy, dies at age 35. Everyone is talking about it, especially your co-worker, John. The first illustration of a conversation with John cuts off communication and diminishes the opportunity for witness, and you miss the meaning John wants to convey.

John: "Wow! Kind of makes you stop and think when a young guy like Andy ups and dies at 35!"

You: "Aw, if you're a Christian, you don't worry about when you die!"

The second illustration of a conversation with John is a positive approach that tries to find the real meaning behind John's words; it is active listening.

John: "Wow! Kind of makes you stop and think when a young guy like Andy ups and dies at 35!"

You: "I'll say. It's kind of scary. What did it make you think about, John?"

John: "About how short life really is and that when our number comes up—'bye-bye.' "

You: "Had you given much thought to 'when your number comes up' prior to Andy's death?"

John: "Not really. When you're young it's the farthest thing from your mind."

47

You: "John, what are some of the things you have been feeling about death since Andy died?"

In this example the method of "effective listening" was to pick up *clues* ("stop and think," "how short life is"), sense a *concern* ("when your number comes up . .."), and then clarify that concern ("How do you feel about death?").

What really was John's concern? What was the meaning that he put into code language in the hope that you would interpret it? John's concern was something like: "I have really started to come to grips with death. Andy's death affected me greatly. I don't want to die. I may fear death more than I realized. I should stop thinking about it."

As I listen to someone's story, I need to listen to the feeling and the real message behind the words that are spoken. I can learn that by practicing "effective listening."

Listening Communicates Acceptance

In Spokane, Washington, a man set up a center named "Let's Talk." He hired several ladies on a commission basis and advertised the center as a place where people will listen to anyone. The initial fee was $15.00 for 30 minutes and $25.00 for an hour. And there is enough business to keep the center open.[2]

Most people want to talk and need to talk about the things they shut up in their minds—worries, concerns, frustrations, disappointments, as well as joys and happiness. We are social beings, and sharing with another person is a natural function.

But to be free enough to share with another person, I must know that that person cares enough about me to take the time and make the effort to listen to me and that he will accept what I say. I can communicate that kind of acceptance by practicing the skills of "effective listening" discussed above and by the body language that communicates silently. The body language includes the movements of my body, how I cross my legs, or twiddle my fingers. It includes the expression on my face, the movement of my eyes, and the tone of my voice as I respond with questions or statements. It can also be in the silence that I permit in the conversation. Someone has suggested that the message I communicate comes 10% through words, 40% through the inflection and tone of my voice, and 50% through facial expression.

Acceptance must be genuine. I accept the other person, no

matter what the person has done. I accept the problem that bothers the other person, no matter how insignificant it may seem. And then I communicate that acceptance by my careful listening and by the way I respond. Kenneth Haugk[3] gives some negative examples:

Don't say: I know just how you're feeling. I lost my job once, too. Don't worry. Just keep looking for something and something will turn up. It always does. It did for me.

Don't say: Don't worry about having a baby. Women have been delivering children since the beginning of time. Once you get that baby in your arms, everything will be just fine.

Do say: I lost my job once, too, and I had some real problems handling it. What are some of the feelings that you have to deal with?

Do say: Having a baby can be an exciting as well as a very anxious time. What are some of the feelings in your mind about it now?

We learn to accept the uniqueness of the problems and feelings of people and accept them as persons. "Unconditional acceptance leads to trust, and trust is closely followed by hope." If a person says, "I hate my mother. I wish she were dead," how would you respond?

Don't say (gasping with shock): "That's terrible. You should not say that."

Do say: "It sounds like you are angry with your mother. (Pause.) Do you want to talk about it?"

The importance of communicating acceptance was demonstrated by Flavil R. Yeakley's[4] study of three kinds of evangelism.

Information transmission: Here a person tells another person the Good News about Jesus Christ in a teacher-student kind of conversation.

Manipulative monolog: This consists of a dialog of sorts but the evangelist retains control of the conversation through prepared questions and statements.

Nonmanipulative dialog: This kind of evangelism consists of two people talking as friends, open to each other and listening to each other. The growth rate of the churches studied indicated that the growth rate of the churches that used the information transmission type of evangelism was very low, the manipulative monolog medium and the nonmanipulative dialog high.

Yeakley discovered that when a new convert perceived the person who led him to faith as a friend, there was a 73% chance that that convert would become an active responsible church member. If the convert saw the person as a salesman, there was an 85% chance that he would become a dropout within the first six months.

I Tell His Story

As I listen to Your Story and as I tell My Story, I am seeking ways to relate both our stories to His Story. His Story is the story of God's love in Jesus Christ, which moved Him to send His only Son to become our brother, take upon Himself our sins, die to pay the penalty for them, and rise again as the conqueror of sin, death, and hell. That's the core of the story. The complete story is much broader than that, of course.

The story of history is His-Story, starting with the creation of the world, of man and woman, and goes through the history of all the nations from the beginning of time. That is God's story, His shaping, directing, ruling, and controlling. His story centers in the cross, where the "great exchange" took place. On the cross Jesus became our sin so that we could receive His righteousness. "He made Him to be sin who knew no sin, so that in Him we might become the righteousness of God" (2 Cor. 5:21). The story goes on after the cross and includes the work of the Holy Spirit in calling, gathering, enlightening, and preserving the church of all believers. It goes on in bringing me in faith and keeping me in faith and in working through the Gospel message in the heart and life of the person to whom I witness.

In order to tell His Story, I need to know His Story. I need to understand it so well that I can summarize it in a way that is logical and makes sense to someone else. For some people it helps to think of the plan of salvation, the core of the story, in terms of an outline like the one used in Dialog Evangelism or Evangelism Explosion: (Grace), Man, God, Christ, Faith. For some it is easier to use the simple outline of passages that describe us as *sinners*, tell how we are *saved*, and then that we are to *serve*. Or one may prefer to use a single passage and give a witness to the Gospel around that passage such as:

John 3:16: "God so loved the world that He gave His only

Son, that whoever believes in Him should not perish but have eternal life."

Eph. 2:8–9: "By grace you have been saved through faith; and this is not your own doing, it is the gift of God—not because of works, lest any man should boast."

Rom. 3:22b–24: "There is no distinction; since all have sinned and fall short of the glory of God, they are justified by His grace as a gift, through the redemption which is in Christ Jesus."

Rom. 6:23: "The wages of sin is death, but the free gift of God is eternal life in Christ Jesus our Lord."

In the previous chapter we discussed the use of tracts as a help to present the way of salvation. Some tracts outline the way of salvation, such as "You Can Be Sure," "A Personal Faith, Now and Forever," or "Seven Important Truths."[5] Another such tract developed by a congregation in Bettendorf, Iowa,[6] uses the Apostles' Creed with supporting Bible passages printed out in a small booklet for this same purpose. The suggestion is to give a copy to someone and then read it with that person. The outline for presenting the way of salvation is the Creed: God the Father, God the Son, and God the Holy Ghost.

A children's book, *The Perfect Friend*, tells the fascinating story of how April tries to witness to her best friend, Margo. April asks her pastor how to do it, and he gives her some Bible passages about the way of salvation. She asks her Sunday school teacher and is advised to "Wait until Margo asks questions and then tell her." April then goes to an older couple and they say, "Tell her to go to church or go to hell." Finally she asks her own father and receives the advice:

"Try to think of what impresses you most about Jesus and touches your heart. Then tell that in your own way to Margo. Nobody can give you the exact words. Just speak out of your love for Jesus. Trust God to help you with the right words at the right time."[7]

Before I tell His Story, I need to listen to Your Story, so that I know where you are in your understanding of His Story and what your need is at this time. Then I seek to tell the particular part of His Story that I sense might be most helpful to you in this moment. I may say:

I know you are really having difficulty accepting the forgiveness that God offers. I find it is important for me to remember that God accepts me for who I am, regardless of how I feel. The story of the prodigal son illustrates for me the forgiving love that God has for us. Would you like me to read that story to you? (Cf. Luke 15:11–32)[8]

Sometimes it is hard to believe that our sins could ever be forgiven. But God has given us his promise to be right there with us even when we find it most difficult to forgive ourselves. The Bible tells us, "If we confess our sins, he is faithful and just, and will forgive our sins and cleanse us from all unrighteousness!" (1 John 1:9)[9]

I was talking to my neighbor, Len, as we each stopped our yard work to visit for a moment. After our first chitchat, Len started to tell me about his brother who had recently died in a nursing home. He shared some of the details of the funeral. I practiced "active listening" as he told me his story. Then I told my story. My brother-in-law had recently died of cancer and Len was interested in some of those funeral arrangements. As we shared our stories, I kept seeking a way to relate our story to His Story. It seemed natural to say something like this very abbreviated transcript:

"I guess we never know, Len, whose turn it is next."

"We just never know, do we?"

"We just keep getting older and sometimes weaker."

"I know what that is. I have a terrible time with these bad knees of mine."

"I'm just glad that when my time comes I know where I am going to go. It kind of takes the sting out of thinking about it."

"I guess we would all like to be sure about where we are going."

"I can be sure because Jesus died on the cross for my sins and promised that He would have a place in heaven reserved for me."

Etc.

To share with another person the Good News that God in his love has provided a way for us to have a full and meaningful life here and now and has promised an even better life in the hereafter, I can use the three-story method. I listen to Your Story, I tell My Story, and I relate our stories to His Story. And I do this in a natural way in normal conversation. That is what the next chapter is about.

For Further Study and Action

1. A Biblical model for personal testimony from St. Paul that uses B.C. and A.D., in addition to the times when St. Paul gave a longer testimony as in Acts 22:3–21 and Acts 26:1–23, is 1 Cor. 6:9–11. What statements does Paul make about B.C. and which about A.D.?

2. Of the five senses—sight, sound, smell, taste, and touch—which ones are specifically mentioned in 1 John 1:1–3? Which are mentioned more than once? What does this say, if anything, about our senses in personal testimony?

3. Try this exercise to help build your witness vocabulary:
   a. Write down all the religious words that you can think of in two minutes.
   b. Check the words that you have used in the last 24 hours.
   c. Go over your list and circle all the words that are "institutional" or "doctrinal" rather than "personal"—e.g., *church, service, hymnal, Bible,* and *justification.*
   d. Draw some conclusions. People often find at least two conclusions: (1) We know more religious words than we use in our daily conversation. They are part of our passive vocabulary and it takes practice to bring them into our active use. (2) We know and often use more institutional words than personal words. How do these conclusions affect our *personal* witness?

4. Write out a personal testimony under the theme, "What Jesus Means to Me." Perhaps you want to focus on one word, e.g., *Savior, Lord, Guide, Friend,* and *forgiveness,* or on a specific Bible verse. You may want to think of the B.C. and A.D. style discussed in this chapter or make a simple statement of what Jesus means to you as you live your life today.

5. Practice the three-story method, using these situations:
   a. Mary announces that her best friend has just admitted to being homosexual.
   b. Tom tells you that his wife is scheduled for surgery.
   c. Peter asks you to go to the ball game with him. He is lonely since his wife left him.

6. Practice the three-story method of witnessing with the one you chose for whom you are praying and to whom you are witnessing, or select another person to add to your list.

4. N for Natural ___

A seminary student was returning on his bicycle from the grocery store to his apartment, carrying his bag of groceries in one arm and steering his bicycle with the other. As he rounded the corner at a busy city intersection, the paper bag split and his groceries spilled all over the pavement. Quickly he laid his bicycle down and began to gather together his edibles before they would be destroyed by the traffic. As he scrambled, he noticed a man standing on the curb on the street corner watching him. "Why doesn't he help me?" the student thought. When the groceries were almost retrieved, the man who was watching stepped off the curb and offered the student a tract on the way of salvation. Needless to say, the student wasn't very receptive to a Gospel witness at that moment!

Our witness should be as natural as possible. The person to whom we witness should not perceive us as standing on a curb, or pedestal, looking down in sympathy and offering a spiritual solution to all our problems. Rather our witness ought to be made in the context of a relationship in which we are perceived as a caring and concerned person. That means that we do not put on a "preachy" tone of voice, or speak about the Gospel only on special occasions and in special places. Our witness needs to be a part of our daily life and conversation.

Witness Is a Life-style

If my witness to the Gospel of Jesus Christ is to be received by the person to whom I speak as a normal part of my conversation, rather than something that I "put on" for special times and places, then it needs to be part of the way I live. It is a part of life-style. My life-style consists of the way I dress and how I use my time; it reflects my priorities and values; it is what I am in the eyes of those who know me and see me every day. My life-style includes the way I speak and how I deal with the problems of life as well as the normal association with others. When my witness is a regular part of that life-style by which people know me, then they receive the words I speak about church or personal faith as authentic. They are natural. People even expect them and anticipate them.

A study in the American Lutheran Church evaluated the data from three separate research projects, *A Study of Generations; Profiles of Lutherans;* and *Portrait of Women of the ALC.* The conclusions indicated that our witness is natural when we live a Christian life. Those who witnessed were in the top 25% of the total sample in neighborliness and in support of others in crisis. Those who witnessed were above the average in personal piety; prayer was very important to their lives and they were in the top 25% in involvement in church and society.

A summary statement made in an unpublished paper describing the results states: "Personal evangelism as performed by Lutherans apparently takes place very naturally and normally in the course of the social interactions of people who are very helpful and neighborly and caring of others, very active in working in the church and community, and surrounded by caring families and congregations. It takes place in the normal social intercourse of working together in church and community and helping friends and acquaintances, and sometimes strangers whenever need becomes apparent."[1]

If my neighbor knows that I attend church regularly and am involved in church and community activities; if he knows that I am always ready to help others, as I see the need, and he knows me as a "good neighbor," he would think it normal that I invite him to come to church with me or that I talk about what I believe. If, however, my neighbor knows that I never attend church or am not interested in community involvement and not very friendly as a neighbor, he might be surprised to hear me talk about religion. And, if he perceives me as a hard man who curses freely, drinks profusely, and at times has wild temper tantrums, he might be completely shocked if I witness to faith in God or he may brush it off as hypocrisy. *Witnessing must be a life-style.*

More evidence of this life-style of witness comes from the studies of the unchurched in the United States. John O'Hara, in looking at a "demographic and psychographic portrait" of the unchurched, suggests that there are between 60 and 80 million unchurched in the United States. While it is true, according to Gallup, that 94% of Americans claim some sort of church affiliation, it is apparent that not all of them are active in a local church.

A 1978 Gallup study of "unchurched" Americans added church attendance as well as affiliation to the definition of "unchurched" and came up with 40% of the population or 61 million, age 18 and over. Another approach used by the *1980 Churches and Church Membership* study counted the actual number of members reported by churches for each county in the United States. These figures were compared with the 1980 census data and the result was an estimated unchurched population of about 50% or 85 million adults.[2]

Why are 60–80 million American adults unchurched? Most of them at one time were in the church or grew up with some contact with the church. A few of them left the church because of doctrinal reasons, some because of conflict with the pastor or another member, but the largest group have left the church and are not in the church today because of "personal convenience." This means that for family or life-style reasons they choose not to be part of a church. John O'Hara summarizes, "There is a significant degree of social distance between the church and the unchurched. The latter have very few friends who are active church members and their spouse, if married, tends to be inactive as well. To a large extent 'churched' and 'unchurched' describe two distinctive subcultures in the U. S. society."[3]

Again the conclusion for us who are seeking to learn better skills in sharing our faith with other people is that witnessing is more than mouthing words. It is a way of life. It includes both my personal devotional life, the kindliness that is expressed in my daily life, and my attitude of care for others. In that context it is natural to speak words of faith.

Witness Is Normal Conversation

When you listen to the normal conversation of people today, whether it be in the car pool, at the office or on the golf course, how religious does it sound? "Our society has become secular" is an oft-heard accusation of critics today. But that is challenged by many who point out that we still have "in God we trust" on our coins, "under God" in our pledge of allegiance to the flag, and use the name of God in oaths sworn in court. Wherever you are in that discussion or debate, the truth is that our conversation has become more secular than it has ever been. "Secular," according to the dictionary, means "pertaining to the world, to things not religious, sacred, or spiritual."

Has it ever been otherwise? When I was a child I remember driving out to grandmother's on Sunday afternoon in the family Model A Ford, all five of us children with Mom and Dad. After a delightful time on the farm, we would pile back in the car to head home to the city and say, "See you next month, Grandma." Her usual response was, "God willing!" I remember both my grandmother and my mother as referring more to God and matters of faith in their normal conversation than I hear most of the time today. And it seemed natural, a normal part of their conversation. That is just the way they talked.

We see the same thing in other cultures. Rev. Edwin T. Brown of Corpus Christi, Texas, writes in an article on witnessing in *The Reporter* that in Spanish it is still the practice to close a visit or conversation with the words, "Vaya con Dios," which means "God go with you," or with "Dios te bandiga," which means "God bless you."[4] What a beautiful custom for Christians to learn and to use as they speak with one another as well as with those who are "unchurched"! This has been a time-honored custom among Christians. The expression "good-bye" came from the expression "God be with you." "God willing" has been used in many languages by Christians for centuries as the familiar Latin testifies, *Deo volente*.

Kenneth Haugk, in his book, *Christian Caregiving: A Way of Life*, speaks of sharing a blessing as a parting at the end of a visit or conversation. The situation, the person's needs, and your own preference determine the kind of "informal benediction" you pronounce at the end of your witness. Examples of such "informal blessings"[5] are

"Peace and joy to you."
"God bless you."
"God be with you."

We may expand the general blessing in order to apply it to a special situation:

"Charlotte, may God shower you with His blessings as you begin your new job out of town. May a sense of His presence be with you always."

Our conversation is a reflection of the thoughts of our mind. If that conversation is to be a witnessing conversation, it must begin with thinking witness, or even more, thinking God. As I am aware of God's presence in my daily life, as I depend on Him and talk to Him in my thoughts, then it is normal and natural for me to speak of Him when I speak to others. If God is not in my thoughts then to put Him in my speech takes a conscious effort which may come through to the other people as something I am now putting on, so it is unnatural and not normal. Some teachers of personal witnessing suggest that I must "think witness" if it is to become a normal part of my conversation. I suggest that I must "think God" and then "think witness."

Witnessing as a normal part of my conversation means that I put into words what is already in my thoughts and mind. If I believe that God is involved in the creation of the world and sustains it by His power; if I believe that He is still Lord of lords and King of kings; if I believe that He is taking care of my life and guiding me day by day, then that can be reflected in the way I speak about the mundane affairs of life. God is involved in them! If I believe it, I say it! I may say it in a lengthy discussion with another person or in a casual conversation. Martin Lundi gives this example:[7]

Jane: "What a beautiful day! I just love springtime!"
You: "Oh, yes. I know exactly what you mean. I especially love the roses. Do you have a favorite?"
Jane: "Not really. I just like everything about spring—the color, the flowers, the trees, everything."
You: "Me, too. It seems like this is the time of year when God is really busy showing His care and concern. He provides new life, new growth, and color to brighten the earth. You're right, it's beautiful!"

It is true that sometimes this kind of brief conversation or reference to my faith is only planting the seed, which someone else may water. Other times it is "setting the stage" or "opening the door" for a future discussion. But if we are living the life of a disciple of Jesus Christ, seeking to be more and more like Him day by day, then our faith is reflected in our conversation in a normal and natural way. If it is not, then something about us is unnatural.

Witness Speaks to a Situation

Witnessing that flows freely from faith needs, however, also to be concerned about the other person and the situation of the conversation. As I use my Q-L-T method (Question-Listen-Tell), I need to practice all the skills I have in active listening in order to understand the other person's story. I try to sense the current need in order to relate our stories to His story. This helps the witness to be received as natural and normal by the person listening.

As I was walking down Broadway in St. Louis one morning on the way to the office about 7:00 a.m., a big fruit truck pulled up to the curb, and the driver rolled down the window. I walked over so we could talk together, and he asked, "Can you tell me how to get to Union Market?" I had to say, "I'm sorry, I can't give you any directions except to say that you might turn at that corner and ask at the service station there. They ought to know." I could have said, "I don't know the way to Union Market, but I do know the way to heaven. Can I tell you about it?" My witness would not have been considered very normal or natural at that point.

A more normal witness that is related to the situation is related by Dr. W. Leroy Biesenthal. As he sat on a plane roaring down the runaway for a takeoff the lady sitting next to him with "knuckles white right up to her elbows" said, "This is where it really gets to me; takeoff and landing." The witness response was "That's when I put my trust in the Lord." This was a simple, natural response to the fear that she had expressed. And Biesenthal says that this opened the door to a floodgate of sharing that didn't stop until the plane touched down an hour later.[8]

One way to learn better how to make a simple witness in a normal way in daily casual conversation is to practice comparing the usual "secular" response to a witness response, such as this:

Statement: "Have a good day."
Secular Response: "You have a good one, too."
Witness Response: "May God give you a good one" or "May God bless your day."

The same can be done with other statements like: "Good Luck!" "Merry Christmas!" "Happy Easter!" or "Thank God it's Friday." Other areas where a similar approach can be used is to think in terms of events or experiences:

Event: First grandchild is born.
Secular Response: "Cute kid." "This is the beginning of second childhood."
Witness Response: "God is so good to let me see my first grandchild. I am going to love that guy and pray for him."

Experience: A daughter runs away to join a cult.

Secular Response: "Too bad. I guess it happens a lot these days."

Witness Response: "I know it must hurt. If there is anything I can do let me know. I will put you and her on my prayer list so that I can regularly ask our loving Lord for guidance and strength."

Sometimes the situation to which the witness must speak is that of a crisis or a hurting moment of life, divorce, sickness, family difficulties, and even death. It is in these kinds of situations that the witness must be sensitive to the feelings of the individual and practice his best listening. Sometimes the best witness that we give in the hurting need of another is our caring and loving presence. That is not to say that we do not speak words, but it is to say that in these situations the words must be the overflow of a caring spirit that is sensed even before the words are heard.

A friend of mine suggests that all one needs to say at times is, "I'm here, and I care." He emphasizes that our presence is a powerful message and will often be more meaningful than an attempt to say something that tries to explain the situation. A witness learns when to speak and when to be silent.

A helpful booklet on how to speak to those in hurting times is one by Kenneth Erickson, *Please Lord, Untie My Tongue.* A good portion of the book warns about what not to do and what not to say. For instance in speaking to one who is sick do not say: "God has a reason for this" or "God allowed this for a purpose."

Erickson suggests that these kinds of statements may be understood as judgmental by the ailing person, and may well be interpreted as evidence of a lack of sensitivity to God's unique involvement in each person's life. Many are the testimonies that follow the pattern quoted here of a person who was seriously ill: "In the middle of the night a nurse took time to listen for a while as I voiced my concerns and worries. She did nothing more than sit on the bed, hold my hand, listen attentively, and be reassuring. This was the turning point of my illness."[9]

Whatever words were spoken by that night nurse, they were received as "reassuring." In times of sickness and death that reassurance comes through caring presence and words that point to God's love. There are different ways to bring the words—greeting cards, Scripture readings, music, and gentle conversation. As one uses the Q-L-T method with the three-story method, even this must be adapted to the situation. As I listen to the patient's story I need to be cautious in "telling my story." A long recital of my operation with all the details may be detrimental rather than helpful. It may be that the more effective "story" that I tell is a brief witness to my personal faith life: "When I was preparing for surgery, the passage of Scripture that was very meaningful to me was Psalm 27. (Would you like for me to read some of it to you?)"

Each of us, I suppose, finds his own way to deal with difficult times. What helps me sometimes is to think about the cross of Jesus Christ and the way that all came about. Through all the scheming of those who put Jesus to death, it was still part of God's plan. He was in charge. And it was His love for us that made it all happen.

The joy of witnessing to people who are in difficult situations is that often they respond with a witness to us and there is a mutual sharing and strengthening of faith. My seating partner on a flight to Kansas City one day was a middle-aged man who, I soon discovered, was from Texas on the way to Kansas City to pick up his two small children, who were with his former wife. He had recently gone through a divorce and had now been awarded the custody of the children. He was going to raise them himself, with the part-time help of his mother. As we talked in a casual way, I tried to catch some of the feeling behind the words he was saying. I knew that marriage counselors tell us that after a marriage breakup people are often filled with feelings of guilt, shame, and failure. I had never been divorced, so I didn't really know. Yet I thought of what this man might be going through: guilt over contribution to the failure of their marriage and regrets for what he didn't do to make the marriage better or for what he did do to help destroy it. And added to these feelings over the past—what about the future?

Surely a man must be apprehensive over the prospect of raising two small children by himself, trying to be both a father and mother, caring for them while keeping a regular job. How do I begin to witness to this situation? I said something like: "I guess it is in times like this one needs some outside help." He quickly responded, "Yes, and I have it. Every night when I go to bed, I put it all in the Lord's hands, and I can sleep without any guilt about the past or any worries about the future." I discovered that he was a Southern Baptist and had a very real faith in Jesus Christ as Savior and Lord of his life. He witnessed more to me than I to him.

Witness in Relationships

Witnessing is a natural part of the conversation of a disciple of Jesus Christ and spoken in normal situations of life as well as crisis situations. It is spoken to those who are a natural part of my life, those closest to me—my family, relatives, and friends. This emphasis on speaking to those closest to me has been called by some writers, such as Win Arn of the American Institute of Church Growth, "*oikos* evangelism." He even calls it, in the title of his book that covers the subject, *The Master's Plan for Making Disciples.*[10]

The word *oikos* is a Greek word that means household. It was used not only for the immediate family but also for the relatives, the servants, and at times friends who lived together as one household. The Gospel was spread in New Testament times through the entire household. When the Roman official knew that his son had been healed by Jesus, he believed "and all his household" (John 4:53). When Peter went to preach to Cornelius, he discovered that Cornelius had gathered all of his relatives and friends to hear (Acts 10). When Lydia was baptized, so was all her household (Acts 16:15). When the jailer at Philippi asked "What must I do to be saved?" Paul told him "Believe in the Lord Jesus, and you will be saved, you and your household" (Acts 16:31). He did, and that very night "he was baptized at once, with all his family" (Acts 16:33).

Win Arn speaks of this witnessing to those who are closest to us as using the "web" principle. There are three webs:

> Common kinship, the large family
>
> Common community, friends and neighbors
>
> Common interests, associates, work relationships, recreation.[11]

Just as a spider web is connected with strands connecting each element, so we are connected to others through one of these common relationships. Our witness is most effective, Arn suggests, when we witness to people in our web, to those with whom we have a connection. Research has shown that each Christian has an average of 8.4 contacts in his web that are unchurched.

The range goes from 12 for those who are new Christians to 4 for those who have been Christians for a long time.

Witnessing to those with whom we have a relationship is the way that the Gospel message was spread from the time when Jesus began his ministry and announced the coming of the kingdom of God. Andrew first found his brother Peter (John 1:40–41). Philip brought his friend Nathanael (John 1:44–45). Matthew brought his tax collector friends (Mark 2:14–15). The healed demoniac was sent home to tell his family and friends "how much God has done for you" (Luke 8:39). Since this was the pattern seen in the ministry of Christ, it was natural for the early church to follow the same pattern with households that believed and were baptized. The conclusion of the historians of the early church is that the church grew primarily through relationships, between friends, families, and neighbors.

Kenneth Scott Latourette, noted church historian, concluded: "The primary change agents in the spread of faith were the men and women who earned their livelihood in some purely secular manner, and spoke of their faith to those whom they met in this natural fashion."[12]

Research that asked thousands of people why they came to Christ and the church indicates that it works the same way today. The following list summarizes the surveys of the American Institute of Church Growth:

> 1–2% special need
> 2–3% walk-ins
> 5–6% pastor
> 1–2% visitation
> 4–5% Sunday school
> ½% evangelistic crusades
> 2–3% church programs
> 75–90% friend or relative.[13]

There is, I suspect, considerable overlap between these reasons that were given by individuals who recently joined the church. The question asked was, "What or who was responsible for your coming to Christ and your church?" How would you answer that? While the person responsible might be a friend or relative, the other factors such as pastor, program, visitation, may have prepared the way for the final consent to come.[14]

It is interesting to compare the reasons why people come to

church in a different culture. One study indicated the following reasons why Japanese first were attracted to the Christian faith:

> 3.8% Christian funerals
> 4.9% weddings
> 6.4% church holidays
> 4.7% missionaries
> 7.2% Christian broadcasts
> 14% family members
> 30% invitation from friends
> 36.7% Christmas or a joyous experience[15]

Putting friends and family members together from the above listing indicates that 44% of the Japanese that were surveyed came to the church because of the influence of friends and relatives. There is again of course some overlap. Who knows how many friends and relatives were related in a smaller way in the other items listed? The point is the same for both the United States and Japan—the large role that friends and relatives play in the paths most people follow in becoming Christians today.

Every study on the influence that led a person to join a church or to come to faith in Christ points in the same direction. In one study of a Billy Graham Crusade, it was discovered that 83% of those who came forward and later joined a church had been brought to the crusade by a friend or relative.

What does this say to me as I seek to witness for my Lord? It suggests, as we summarize the emphasis of this chapter:

1. Witnessing is not only words, it is a life-style.

2. Witnessing can be a part of normal conversation when it reflects the thoughts and attitudes of a person living in fellowship with God.

3. The witness listens to the needs and hurts of the person to whom he speaks and tries to apply the Gospel to those needs and hurts.

4. The witness begins with those closest—family, relatives, and friends—and then reaches out to others as there is opportunity.

With these points guiding my witness, it can be natural and normal. Everyone who is a disciple of Jesus Christ is a witness of Jesus Christ. That is what we will discuss further in the next chapter.

For Further Study and Action

1. Read the story of Cornelius in Acts 10. When Cornelius was expecting Peter, what did he do (vv. 24, 27)? Does this suggest a way in which we might witness to our friends and neighbors?
2. Look up these additional examples of how people came to faith through webs of family and friends:

   > Zacchaeus: Luke 19:9
   > Crispus: Acts 18:8
   > Stephanas: 1 Cor. 1:16
   > The sinful woman and others: Luke 7:37–8:3

3. If you are in a class, ask other members of the class to share how they came to faith in Jesus and to this church.
4. Christians like to be with Christians. So then they often do not have many non-Christian friends. The number of unchurched friends usually drops the longer one is a Christian, from 12 to 4. Discuss the possibilities of deliberately making friends with an unchurched person in order to witness to that person.
5. Practice witnessing in daily life situations by comparing a "secular response" to a "witness response" for the following:

An event	Secular Response	Witness Response
a. Going on a trip		
b. Anniversary		

A Statement
   a. Thank God it's Friday
   b. It's raining again

A Situation
   a. Retirement
   b. Layoff

An Activity
   a. Going on vacation
   b. Job change

An Experience
   a. Close call in a car
   b. Lost money in house sale

6. Spend some time with the friend(s) to whom you are witnessing and for whom you are praying. Try to find ways to make a simple witness response to situations like those above.

5. E for Everyone ___

When our son David was six years old, I would bring home a small gift whenever I was gone away for a few days for a conference or workshop. One time in an airport shop I found a T-shirt that had the picture of a little boy with a halo around his head and the words printed out, "I'm a good angel." When I gave it to David, he liked it. But my wife thought that it wouldn't be the best thing to wear to school, because of what others might say. So she insisted that David wear it as an undershirt, so there would always be another shirt over it.

Shortly after giving David his "I'm a good angel" T-shirt, our neighbor lady across the street died after an extended bout with cancer. This lady's daughter, Jeannie, was David's regular baby-sitter when my wife and I were gone in the evening. We told David when he came home from school that Jeannie's mother died. He didn't say much and was rather quiet the rest of the afternoon. After supper I went to my study in the basement, and David came to me there with a request. "Daddy, would you write a note to Jeannie for me?" He dictated, and I wrote:

Dear Jeannie:

I'm sorry your mother died. I hope that she is now happy in heaven.

Then he printed his name as only a first-grader can, folded the note, also as first-graders do, and personally delivered it across the street to Jeannie. As I watched him go to the door, I thought, Maybe no one can read his T-shirt, but right now he really is a good angel.

A witness is a good angel, one who is a messenger for Jesus Christ bringing to others the Good News of forgiveness of sins and new life in Him. And everyone is an angel! Everyone, that is, who is a follower of Jesus Christ, who knows Him as personal Savior and serves Him as the Lord of life.

All Disciples Are Witnesses

We need to go back to where we began, Acts 1:8, and summarize a few of the things that we discussed in chapter 1. Forty days after His resurrection Jesus took His disciples to the hill where He spoke His last words. The disciples still expected Him to establish His kingdom on earth in Israel, and He had to rebuke them once more: "It is not for you to know times or seasons which the Father has fixed by his own authority." He wanted to shift their thinking from receiving honor and power in a physical kingdom to the power that they would receive in order for them to be involved in establishing God's kingdom in the hearts and lives of people. They would do that by telling the world about Jesus Christ. So Jesus said as He sought to change the direction of their thinking, "You shall receive power when the Holy Spirit has come upon you; and you shall be My witnesses in Jerusalem and in all Judea and Samaria and to the end of the earth."

"Shall be" is the future tense, as these words are recorded by the historian Luke, which has a present meaning. While "we shall" looks like a future action, it has present intent. It is like saying, as the rabbinic law says, "Every child born of a Jewish mother will be a Jew." When will the child be a Jew? When he is bar mitzvahed at age 13? When he learns Hebrew? No, but when he is born of a Jewish mother he is automatically considered to be a Jew. He is a Jew by birth.

That is what Jesus is saying to His disciples. As a disciple you are My witness. When you were born the second time you became My disciple and My witness. Jesus was, of course, speaking to those who had seen Him in person, had heard His teaching, seen His miracles, witnessed His death and His resurrection. They were truly witnesses, and could tell the world what they had "seen and heard" (Acts 4:20). In a secondary sense, all those who became disciples through the preaching and teaching of those first witnesses also became witnesses, to tell what they had "seen and heard" through the testimony of the apostles as recorded in the Scripture. It is in that sense that we say today, everyone who is a disciple of Jesus Christ is a witness. (See chapter 1 for a further discussion.)

We use the word disciple because that is the Biblical word for a follower of Jesus Christ. The word *Christian* was first used by the enemies of Christ as a term of derision for the followers of Christ. It appears in the New Testament only three times: Acts 11:26; 26:28; and 1 Peter 4:16. The word *disciples*, while used about 30 times to refer to the Twelve, is used over 260 times in the four gospels and the book of Acts. It is used of those who are "disciples of Moses" (John 9:28), "John's disciples . . . disciples of the Pharisees" (Mark 2:18; cf. Matt. 22:16), and disciples of Jesus and of John the Baptist (Luke 11:1). *Disciple*, as used among the Greeks, was one who followed the teachings of another. It is used this way in some New Testament passages, as in referring to the disciples of Moses or the Pharisees. Jesus, however, added a new dimension to the word when He included the personal relationship between teacher and disciple in which the disciple looks to the teacher as Lord and seeks to become like Him.

In this chapter we prefer to use the term *disciple*, rather than *Christian*, because of the deeper Biblical meaning of the word. A disciple of Jesus Christ is one who has been chosen and called by God, who has been born the second time, born into the kingdom of God. A disciple serves Jesus Christ as Lord, seeking to become more and more like Him, and sees his purpose in life to be a discipler of others. He "follows in His train," one hymn puts it, and in that of all the disciples who have gone before. He is part of that movement of disciples who spread the Good News, so that like ripples on water it moves out in an ever broadening circle, as Jesus puts it, from Jerusalem, to "all Judea and Samaria and to the end of the earth" (Acts 1:8).

All the disciples of Jesus Christ are witnesses, even though not all of them actively witness. But as we said in chapter 1, a disciple of Jesus Christ is a witness whether he wants to be or not. When he identifies with the name of Jesus Christ and His church, he is a witness. Every disciple is on the witness stand. What he says or does not say, what he does or does not do is his witness. Many who identify themselves as Christians and as church members do not see themselves as witnesses to others but prefer to make their faith a private matter. This is evidenced by the surveys that show that only about half of the Christians today give a verbal witness.

In one survey, a cross section of people from several denominations were asked two questions: (1) Have you ever tried to get anyone to join your religious group? (2) Did you ever succeed in getting anyone to join? The results were as follows:[1]

	1. *Tried* (%)	2. *Succeeded* (%)
Baptists	67	50
Congregationalists	32	19

Episcopalians	53	45
Lutherans	49	28
Methodists	56	39
Presbyterians	59	52
Roman Catholics	28	17
Other Protestants	61	44

In a study of all the Lutherans in the United States, those surveyed were asked about their witnessing with the questions:[2] "During the past year I have . . .

a. Invited a non-Christian to my church or Sunday school.

b. Invited another Christian to my church or Sunday school.

c. Visited someone's home to share the Gospel.

d. Distributed Christian tracts.

e. Made a specific declaration of my personal faith to a friend.

f. Made a specific declaration of personal faith to a stranger.

Of 5,000 Lutherans surveyed, 50% never witnessed once during the past year; 40% did it "seldom"; and 10% did it often.[3] A follow-up study among Lutherans in 1980 resulted in similar figures. In this study, 53% of those surveyed did not witness to a stranger in the last year, and 10% did witness four or more times. This study also asked about witnessing to acquaintances, friends, and family, in that order, and the witnessing increased in each category. Significant, however, was the fact that of those who did witness, 56% felt uncomfortable in doing so even among friends and acquaintances.[4]

All of these studies, together with others, lead to the general conclusion that many Christians, in fact up to 50% in some denominations, do not witness regularly. They do not invite others to their church nor tell them about Jesus Christ nor share their personal faith. Perhaps that is one of the reasons why the Christian church in the United States has not been growing as rapidly as we see it grow in some other parts of the world. We praise God for those faithful disciples who do witness regularly and seek to motivate and equip others to join them. Above all, the church must continue to teach the Biblical truth that all disciples of Jesus Christ are witnesses for Jesus Christ.

A missionary once asked a young convert, "How many have you brought to Jesus since you became a Christian?"

"Oh," said the young convert, "I am just a learner and didn't even possess a complete New Testament until yesterday."

The missionary responded, "Do you use candles in your home?"

After an affirmative reply, the missionary continued, "Do you expect the candle to begin to shine only after it is burned halfway down?"

"No, of course not. It shines as soon as it is lit." The young man saw the point and within a short time he had brought several friends and neighbors to the mission with him.

After Jesus told his first disciples, "You shall be My witnesses" (Acts 1:8), He did tell them to wait awhile before they began the work. They were to go back to Jerusalem and wait until they received the power to witness that would come when they received the Holy Spirit. That happened on Pentecost, after they had waited and prayed for 10 days. We will discuss the motivation to witness later in this chapter, but first we need to explore a little further the concept that all disciples not only *are* witnesses, but all disciples *can* witness, even though they may not be doing it now.

All Disciples Can Witness

The Christian church looks to the day of Pentecost as its birthday. On that day the Holy Spirit was poured out on the disciples to give them power to witness. As they witnessed, 3,000 came to believe and were baptized. After Pentecost the church continued to grow, as recorded in the Book of Acts:

Acts 2:41—3,000 believe and are baptized.

Acts 2:47—The Lord adds daily to the church.

Acts 4:4—The number has grown to 5,000 men, not counting women and children.

Acts 5:14—Multitudes of men and women are added.

Acts 6:1—The number of disciples continues to increase.

Acts 9:31—The church was strengthened and grew in numbers.

Acts 16:5—"The churches were strengthened in faith, and they increased in numbers daily."

As the church exploded, the Jewish leaders watched in amazement and "jealousy" (Acts 5:17). They thought they had rid the country of this sect—which followed Jesus of Nazareth—when they had Him crucified, and now it was growing out of control. They tried to stop it, arresting the leaders and forbidding them to teach about Jesus. But Peter and John responded, "We

70

must obey God rather than men. . . . We are witnesses to these things, and so is the Holy Spirit whom God has given to those who obey him" (Acts 5:27–32). Stephen, one of the six deacons, was stoned to death, and "a great persecution arose against the church in Jerusalem" (Acts 8:1).

That persecution helped the ripple effect mentioned in Acts 1:8. Acts 8:1 records that because of the persecution "they were all scattered throughout the region of Judea and Samaria," and the writer, Luke, tacks on to that verse the provocative phrase, "except the apostles." The apostles saw their task as working in Jerusalem even though the others left. Who left? The believers, those who were not the apostles, those we often call the lay people of the church. These are the ones that were scattered and who, according to the account, spread the Gospel in Judea and Samaria. "Now those who were scattered went about preaching the word" (Acts 8:4). The word translated "preaching" in that verse is the Greek word *euangelizomai*, from which our English word "evangelism" comes. As mentioned previously, this word, as it is used in the New Testament, means telling the Good News about Jesus Christ. The lay people did not set up street-corner services or build pulpits to preach. They talked about Jesus Christ to their neighbors across the back fence, to the people they met at the market and their new place of work. It was a normal part of their conversation. One might say "they gossiped the Gospel." It was part of their daily life and talk. Their walk and their talk centered in Jesus Christ.

All the disciples of Jesus Christ *are* witnesses, and they *can* witness. Whether one is a called professional church worker or a "regular" member of the church, part of the "vocation" of every Christian is to be a witness for the Lord Jesus. As Peter puts it, every disciple is a "royal priest" whose purpose is to "declare the wonderful deeds of Him who called you out of darkness into His marvelous light" (1 Peter 2:9).

Luther championed the general priesthood of all believers and, as the theologian-historian Philip Schaff puts it, "This principle implies the right and duty of every believer to read the Word of God in his vernacular tongue, to go directly to the throne of grace, and to take an active part of all the affairs of the church according to his particular gift and calling."[5] We need to add to that definition, especially in the part about being involved in the "affairs of the church." Part of the ministry of every Christian priest is to declare the marvelous works of the almighty God in reconciling the world to Himself and offering that reconciliation to others. Luther calls Christians "eitel Roehren," empty channels or pipelines through which flow His light and life into men "sitting in darkness and in the shadow of death."[6] We cannot supply the grace that God sends flowing through us, but we can block the flow. We can shut off the witness stream.

Everyone, every disciple of Jesus Christ, is a witness—every man, woman, and child, in whatever place in life or occupation one finds oneself. It is only when all the disciples of Jesus Christ function as the priests that they are, and share their faith with others as the witnesses that they are, that the church will fulfill its mission and many will become disciples. The key to the evangelization of the world, Paul Foust suggests, however, is the lay people, and the key to the lay people is held by the clergy. The clergy, through the public use of the means of grace, i.e., preaching the Gospel and administering the sacraments, are to build up the body of Christ, motivate, and equip the lay people for their task of witnessing. But Foust feels the lay people are the answer for world evangelization because:

1. There are more of them! (600 times as many)

2. They are where the unbelieving world is, working right beside them everyday.

3. They stay with the candidate for the Kingdom and can follow through.

4. Their witness is more readily trusted. They are satisfied customers rather than paid salesmen.

5. "Every Christian a witness" is God's system.[7]

All disciples are witnesses, even though all of them are not actively giving a positive witness. But it is possible to help those who are not witnessing. They can be led to grow in faith and life, be taught some skills as to how to begin talking about their faith. And they can be motivated by the Gospel to grow in their desire to witness. A young man who served his Lord in the mission field of New Guinea once said, "Every Christian either is a missionary or needs one."[8]

All Disciples Can Be Motivated

I was sharing a cab from a hotel in downtown Kansas City to the airport to catch a plane back to St. Louis and discovered that the young man I was riding with worked with blind-deaf children. I was interested in how a child who is both blind and deaf can learn, how they can communicate with us and we with them. So I was emphasizing the Q and L in the Q-L-T method (Question-Listen-Tell). Finally after hearing about the problems and frustrations of this kind of work, I asked, "Why do you do it?" My companion thought a moment and then said, "I guess because of the satisfaction I get out of seeing a child respond even a little." I had to confess, "I don't think that would be enough for me." When he asked me why I was a minister I confessed that it was because I believe God called me to be one and "I do it out of love for my Lord Jesus."

Why should Christians witness? Why should they put themselves on the line, expose themselves to the ridicule and rejection of the world? How can they be motivated to witness despite the barriers? That is the big problem. We have seen that only half of all Christians do any witnessing at all. Could that be why most denominations are not growing but are on a plateau or even declining?

Different reasons have been given for the membership losses in the churches in the 1970s. Researchers David A. Rosen and Dean R. Hoge suggest the primary factors are "cultural forces external to the church." Dean Kelly insists that it is the lack of a unitary set of beliefs and a distinctive life-style that growing conservative churches had. Merton P. Strommen, however, after reviewing these claims, gives his opinion that the primary reason centers in the "life and theology of the congregation." He says the "compelling need among us" is "a lack of urgency and evangelistic concern for people outside the faith."[9] He cites a survey in which lay and clergy alike were asked to identify the 6 most important functions of the congregation out of a list of 14 possibilities. First priority given by 71% was attending the Sunday morning worship. Less than 2% identified evangelism and supporting members in times of need as important enough to be in the top six.[10]

A friend admitted to me, "I am concerned about those outside the faith but I too often lack the 'urgency' to witness and my motivation needs bolstering." What does it take to "bolster" the motivation, to give witnessing a higher priority? As I listen to lectures and sermons and as I have searched the writings of others on how speakers and authors seek to motivate to witness, I find much confusion. One writer, Elmer Kettner, several decades ago gave these five reasons to answer the question, Why evangelize?

1. That's why God has called you into His kingdom.
2. Your lost fellowmen need your testimony.
3. You can witness to the wonderful works of God.
4. God will help you to do so.
5. You'll be glad you did.[11]

In more recent writings I find that the appeals being used today might be summarized in these five words: duty, pity, obligation, privilege, love. We will examine each of them a little more in detail.

1. *It is my duty to witness.*

The authors who use "It is my duty" as the main thrust in trying to motivate people to witness speak of obedience to the command of the Lord. "You shall be My witnesses" (Acts 1:8). "Make disciples of all nations" (Matt. 28:20). "As the Father has sent me, even so I send you" (John 20:21). I am the servant and I must obey my master.

2. *Pity the condition of the lost.*

"He who does not believe will be condemned" (Mark 16:16). That means eternal suffering in hell. If my neighbor or relative does not come to believe in Jesus Christ as Savior, he will go to hell for all eternity. "You will die in your sins unless you believe that I am He," Jesus said (John 8:24). If no one finds the lost sheep, it will not find its own way back. Perhaps I am the only one who can bring a particular lost sheep into the fold.

3. *It is your obligation.*

St. Paul said that he had an obligation to preach the Gospel to all people, since God had saved him and called him to be an apostle to the Gentiles. "I am under obligation both to Greeks and to barbarians, both to the wise and to the foolish: so I am eager to preach the gospel to you also who are in Rome" (Rom. 1:14–15).

A man came to his pastor one day to ask him to pray for him that he might find a different job. The pastor asked, "Don't you like your work?"

"Oh, I like my work fine," the man replied.

"Aren't you getting enough money for your work?" the pastor continued to question.

"Yes, I think I am getting good wages," came the reply.

"Why then do you want to move?" asked the pastor, having difficulty understanding the situation.

"Because I am the only Christian in the shop, and I get hungry for Christian fellowship," he explained.

The pastor responded. "I'm going to pray against you. You have a great opportunity to witness if none of the rest of the men are Christian. Perhaps that is where God wants you to be, so that you can witness to them."

4. *It is your privilege to share Jesus Christ.*

It is a privilege to know Jesus Christ as Savior. He gives peace by forgiving all sins. He helps you to deal with the problems of daily life. He is your close friend and companion and He has promised that there is even a better life waiting for you after this one. Because Jesus Christ does so much for you, don't you want to share Him with others?

Do these four appeals motivate you? There is nothing wrong with any of them, and proper Christian motivation involves all of them in some fashion. The problem is that each of these points from 1 through 4 are at times used as Law approaches that try to motivate disciples by the pressure of "ought" and "must" and "should." The Law cannot motivate. It can make us feel guilty for what we have not done. It is only the Gospel of Jesus Christ that can make us want to witness, make us want to share Jesus Christ. But our motivations are complex. More than one factor is at work at the same time. Take the example of Lars Monson.

Lars went to see his brother Al in the hospital on a Sunday afternoon. He thought: He's fading fast with emphysema, and I don't think he's ready to meet his Maker. His brother was confirmed many years before but didn't have much to do with the church since that time. Now as Lars watched his brother struggle for oxygen from tubes, he realized that his brother needed more than the breath of life; he needed the breath of eternal life. Lars's mind went back to their boyhood days on the farm—duck hunting, chores, and picking strawberries. Then he remembered confirmation day and the promises made that day. By the grace of God, Lars had kept his promises but his brother had not. Now Al lay dying and Lars knew he had to do something. So, although he had never made a verbal witness to his brother before, he started to talk to Al and his wife about Jesus, forgiveness, and eternal life.[12]

What made Lars break his silence and finally witness to his

brother? He felt a concern for the eternal destination of his brother's soul. He wanted desperately to see his brother in heaven. Many motivations were at work, of both Law and Gospel orientation. The motivation we seek, even though it may often be mixed with others, is what St. Paul summed up in the little phrase, "the love of Christ controls." (2 Cor. 5:14)

5. *The love of Christ controls.*

In writing to the Corinthian congregation, Paul emphasized that if anyone is in Christ he is a "new creation; the old has passed away, . . . the new has come" (2 Cor. 5:17). It is this "new creation," in whom the old nature has died and the new life of the Spirit has come, that is "controlled" by the love of Christ (2 Cor. 5:14). Other translations use the words "constrains" or "rules." This new creation in Christ is the work of the Holy Spirit. Just as St. Paul said that "no one can say 'Jesus is Lord' except by the Holy Spirit" (1 Cor. 12:3), so no one can share his faith in the Lord with another person except by the power of the Holy Spirit at work in him. That is why Jesus told His disciples to wait in Jerusalem until they received the "power from on high" (Luke 24:49) before beginning their witness. That power came when they were filled with the Holy Spirit.

Before Pentecost the apostles were hiding behind locked doors. After Pentecost they stood in the temple and called all people to repentance and baptism. Before Pentecost they ran away from the leaders of the Jewish people. After Pentecost they stood before the same court that sent Jesus to Pilate and to His death and accused them of killing the Son of God. And when the Sanhedrin threatened them and commanded that they stop preaching, they defied them and said, "We must obey God rather than men" (Acts 5:29). The motivation to witness is the Spirit of God at work in us, who is constantly renewing us and making us "new creatures" (cf. 2 Cor. 5:17) controlled by the love of Christ.

Often when I go past the Old Court House in downtown St. Louis and see the broad porch areas, I think of the slave auctions that once were held there. The reason I think about that so often is the story of the freeing of a slave. A man's bid held. After he paid the price, the slave dutifully began to follow him. The man turned to the slave and said, "You are free. I bought you to set you free. You may go." The slave didn't know what to do. Finally he stammered, "Sir, I would like to be your slave for the rest of my life."

In a small way that illustrates what happens to the disciple of Jesus Christ. He has been bought with the blood of Jesus Christ, God's Son. He is free from the power of sin, death, and hell. In love and gratitude he bows before his Master, Jesus, and says, "I want to be Your slave." He is controlled by love for Him. That is why he tells others about Him.

All Disciples Can Find Opportunities to Witness

Every disciple of Jesus Christ is a witness. A disciple can witness, a disciple can be motivated to witness, and now we add this to the list, that every disciple can find opportunities to witness. Just as each one of us does not witness in the same way, because we are different persons with different gifts and abilities, so we all have different places and opportunities to witness. But all of us have opportunities as long as we live in relationship with other people. And the Holy Spirit leads us to recognize and use those opportunities.

Oscar Feucht, in *Everyone a Minister*, speaks about "six sectors of service" in which a Christian functions in his vocation as a priest. Looking at the six sectors can help us to think of the places and opportunities where we are to witness.[13]

1. *The Personal Sector*. This involves our personal relationship to God, the pursuit of personal goals, the practice of prayer, and the use of Scripture. This is our whole philosophy of life, reflected in our words and deeds, both in and out of the Christian fellowship.

2. *The Family Sector*. In relationship to our spouse, children, brothers, and sisters, we express our calling to serve God and each other. We fulfill roles as teachers, devotional leaders, counselors, and enablers.

3. *The Congregational Sector*. The church is our "alma mater," our nourishing mother. We both receive from her and give to her. It is here that we use our gifts for her welfare and she equips us to witness and serve.

4. *The Community Sector*. Every parish is to be a social service center as well as an evangelistic center. We have a calling to the neighbors down the street and to the poor and disadvantaged. Here we are the light, leaven, and salt of the earth.

5. *The Occupational Sector*. The disciple is to be "visible" on

his job by the manner of conversation, the language he uses, the spirit in which he does his work, and the fairness and consideration he expresses to his fellow workers and his boss. "He witnesses on his job by what he says, by how he works, by honest workmanship, and by his concern for his fellow workers."

6. *The Civic-Political Sector*. The Christian's vocation involves his civic-mindedness, his interest in human rights and equal employment opportunities, and even his readiness to serve in public office.

In this broad spectrum of the Christian's vocation, the disciple finds opportunities to witness to Jesus Christ in his own way and his own style. A prominent American clergyman is reported to have said to the New York State Legislature: "I'm not going to pray for you. There are certain things a man does for himself. He has to blow his own nose, make his own love, and say his own prayers."[14] To that list we could add, "make his own witness." No one can make your witness for you. You are a unique person, called and gifted by God, and placed in situations where only you can give a Christian witness. Look at some examples of how people have found ways to witness in their own corner of the world.

A doctor in LaCrosse, Wisconsin, as he visits patients in the hospital, especially on the night before surgery, carries a New Testament and some tracts in the pocket of his gown. As he prepares the patients for surgery by explaining what will happen and answering any questions the patient has, he also witnesses to the patient and, when appropriate, leaves the tract, "When Facing an Operation,"[15] or a New Testament.

A taxi driver in Asheville, North Carolina, carried a Bible in the cab on his seat, so that, when he waited for fares, he could read a little. A medical doctor who took his cab one day noticed the Bible and asked him about it. Together the two of them started a ministry. They left Bibles in the back seats of cabs and developed an apron that could be tied to the back of the driver's seat and that held the booklet "Jesus," published by the American Bible Society.

A lady invites neighbor ladies in for morning coffee, so that she not only has a chance to meet them but to witness to them.

A man who doesn't care much to hunt, took up the sport, so that he could become closer friends with two men he worked with and would have time to witness to them on their hunting trips.

A child came home from kindergarten with a piece of paper on which were circles and squares. The mother asked, "Are you learning to count in kindergarten?"

"No," said the girl, "these are the seats of the boys and girls in my class. Those marked with an X in the squares go to church; those with circles do not."

The mother asked, "How did you find out?"

"I asked them," the child replied. "And I invited them to come to our church."

This little girl had found her own way to witness and found prospects for the church in doing it. Perhaps some of us have acquaintances who do not go to church, or perhaps we do not know whether or not they do. The little girl had a good idea. Ask them. That is one way.

In concluding this chapter, perhaps it does need to be said that while every disciple is a witness and can witness, some can do it, humanly speaking, better than others. Those whose personality allows them to be at ease in socializing with all kinds of people, may find it a little easier to relate to people and develop relationships in which they can witness with both their lives and their lips. Those who are more facile with their tongue and are accustomed to speaking may find it easier to verbalize their faith because they are used to talking about everything else. Where does that leave the person who finds it difficult to socialize and to whom conversation does not come easily?

Each disciple of Jesus Christ first needs to find the spiritual gift or gifts the Lord has given and develop them through use in the church. Then as the gifts are being used to build the body of Christ, that disciple grows in faith and love and learns how to express faith and to share it with others. This may be a slow development and a very simple witness, but it can be learned as the Spirit of God leads.

There are no requirements for a witness except to be a disciple of Jesus Christ. My witness does not have to use certain words or cover all the subjects of the catechism. By God's Spirit at work in me, I can sow a few seeds that others may water and for which God can give the increase. I can Q-L-T (Question-Listen-Tell). I am not responsible for the results of my witness, although I pray for them. God gives the results in His own way and His own time. We will discuss that further as we move into the next two chapters.

For Further Study and Action

1. Examine the three times in the Bible where the word "Christian" appears and note the context of each passage. Is the word used the same way each time or is there a difference?

    Acts 11:26 _____

    Acts 26:28 _____

    1 Peter 4:16 _____

2. For a longer study, read the book of Acts and underline the words used for believers of Christ and note how often each word is used: Christian, disciple, brother, church.

3. Examine your own motivation for witnessing, as discussed in this chapter. Prioritize the key words, marking from 1 to 5, 1 being the word that is most meaningful to you and 5 the one that is least. Compare your list with that of others. What accounts for the differences?

    _____Duty

    _____Pity

    _____Obligation

    _____Privilege

    _____Love

4. You are having coffee in a restaurant with a friend and the conversation turns to religion. He says, "I think it really doesn't matter what a person believes so long as he is sincere." How would you respond?

5. Mahatma Gandhi is reported to have said that Christian witness ought to be like the aroma of a roast in the oven, wafting out on the streets of India and drawing in hungry beggars irresistibly. What is the aroma that draws?

    2 Cor. 2:15 _____

    John 13:35 _____

    1 Thess. 3:12 _____

    Luke 10:25–37 _____

6. Every disciple is on the witness stand and must always be ready to answer when asked. How does Peter suggest that the disciple give his answer? 1 Peter 3:15.

7. Think about the special person for whom you are praying and to whom you are witnessing. What motivates you to be concerned for that person?

6. S for Save

The primary author of Schwan's catechism, the Rev. Henry C. Schwan, was pastor of St. Paul Lutheran Church, Cleveland, Ohio, for almost 50 years. Dr. Herman Gockel tells the story that each year when Pastor Schwan prepared his confirmation class for their public examination he would drill them to answer specific questions. It was all in German in those days of course. One question he used year after year was this:

"Warum sind wir Menschen denn hier auf Erden?" (Why are we here on earth?)

With push-button response the answer would come from the class as it had been taught, "Um in dem Himmel zu kommen." (In order to go to heaven.)

Surely, going to heaven is the ultimate destiny, the final fulfillment of the hope of every Christian, to claim the place reserved in the mansions that Jesus has prepared (John 14:2–4). St. Paul even says "My desire is to depart and be with Christ" (Phil. 1:23). As soon as we are baptized into Christ, we are in the family of God, and our home is heaven, the home of our Father, the place where we belong. But God doesn't take us to our home the moment that we are baptized or come to faith in Jesus Christ. He leaves us here on earth as "aliens and exiles" (1 Peter 2:11). And He does that for a special purpose. He has work for us to do for Him on earth, and we are the only ones who can do it according to His plan and design. We are the instruments by which God accomplishes His purpose.

Christ Came to Save the Lost

In this chapter we will look at our purpose for being on earth in terms of the word *save*. Jesus summed up his ministry with the word *save*: "The Son of man came to seek and to save the lost" (Luke 19:10). St. Paul described that saving the lost as "reconciling the world" when he said, "In Christ God was reconciling the world to himself" (2 Cor. 5:19). That purpose was finished when Jesus Christ rose from the dead and returned to His

Father who had sent Him. He reported, "mission accomplished." But before He left the earth Jesus commissioned His followers to carry on that mission, to continue to seek out the lost in the world and tell them that they have been reconciled. The Scriptures record the assigning of that task with a number of different expressions. Jesus said, "As the Father has sent Me, even so I send you" (John 20:21). St. Paul uses the phrase "entrusting to us the message" and "gave us the ministry of reconciliation" (2 Cor. 5:18–19). The words in Matthew's Gospel are "make disciples of all nations" (Matthew 28:19–20). Before we examine our assignment to continue the mission of Jesus to seek and save the lost, we need to examine the word "lost" and the word "save."

The basic meaning of the word "lost" is to go astray. One who is lost has left the place where he belongs. The sheep that left the flock is lost, and the shepherd goes to find it (Luke 15:3–6). The woman searches the house until she finds the lost coin (Luke 15:8–9). In the parable of the prodigal son, the father says when his son returns, "This my son was dead, and is alive again; he was lost, and is found" (Luke 15:24). These words of the father illustrate what the Bible means by being "lost." When one is "lost" he is "dead." Another word that is used is *perish*. The Gospel-in-a-nutshell passage, John 3:16, uses the word "perish" in this way. God sent His son, so that whoever believes in Him will not "perish" but have eternal life. Jesus told His disciples, when He sent them out on their first assignment, not to go to the Gentiles or to any towns of the Samaritans, but rather "to the lost sheep of the house of Israel" (Matt. 10:6). Paul speaks of the unbelievers as those who "are perishing" (2 Cor. 4:3).

The lost are dead in their trespasses and sins. They are reaping the reward of their sins. "The soul that sins shall die" (Ezek. 18:4). "The wages of sin is death" (Rom. 6:23). This death is a separation from God, an alienation from the fellowship with God for which we were created. The final result of this death is eternal separation from God in hell, described in the New Testament as the place of suffering that was originally prepared for the devil and his angels. Jesus will say on judgment day to those on His left, "Depart from me, you cursed, into the eternal fire prepared for the devil and his angels" (Matt. 25:41).

Sin sends us to hell! That is the message of Jesus and the apostles. Jesus warns about going to hell in such strong language that He even suggests that if my hand or foot causes me to sin and go to hell, then it would be better to cut it off and escape hell, or even to pluck out my eye if that were the cause of my going to hell. He concludes, "It is better for you to enter the kingdom of God with one eye than with two eyes to be thrown into hell, where their worm does not die, and the fire is not quenched" (Mark 9:47–48). Jesus warns that hell is a place of eternal suffering for the sins that we have committed here on earth. To be destined for that suffering is to be lost. The only way to escape that fate is for someone to find me and save me.

Some years ago I read about the submarine named *Thresher* that sank in the ocean and could not surface. I thought of the people in that submarine and how they must have felt. Perhaps for a time they tried to bolster their spirits by hoping that something might "fix" their ship and get them back to the surface. Surely they soon realized, however, that the only way they could be rescued or saved is if someone came down from above and rescued them. That is the way it is with every human being, born with inherited sin that makes him "dead" (Eph. 2:1), "hostile to God" (Rom. 8:7), a slave of sin (cf. Rom. 6:2), and doomed unless someone comes down from above to rescue him. Jesus came to do that, "to seek and to save the lost" (Luke 19:10). So Peter tells the Sanhedrin, "There is salvation in no one else, for there is no other name [than Jesus] under heaven given among men by which we must be saved" (Acts 4:12).

The New Testament Greek word that is translated "save" is *sōzō*. It is used to refer to being saved or delivered from danger, suffering, sickness, or in a spiritual sense from being lost in sin. It is the giving of life to those who are dead. It is the freeing of those who are slaves. The angel Gabriel, who told Mary that she would be the mother of the Messiah, said, "You shall call His name Jesus" (Luke 1:31). *Jesus* is a Greek word that means "one who saves." It is akin to the Hebrew word *Joshua*, which means "Yahweh saves" or "Yahweh delivers." So the angel of the Lord who spoke to Joseph in a dream explained, "You shall call His name Jesus, for He will save His people from their sins" (Matt. 1:21).

When the apostles on and after Pentecost preached the Gospel, using the phrase of "be saved," people understood what they meant. In his Pentecost sermon Peter quoted the prophet Joel, "Whoever calls on the name of the Lord shall be saved" (Acts 2:21) and then urged those who were listening, "Save yourselves" (Acts 2:40). After the 3,000 were baptized, Luke says, "The Lord added to their number day by day those who were being saved" (Acts 2:47).

Today the word *save* still has abundant meaning to those who are saved, to the Christians. But to the world the concept of being saved has little meaning. John Wimber grew up in Peoria, Illinois, with no connection to the church whatsoever. He tells audiences to whom he now speaks as a Church Growth leader that, when he was a teenager, he would ride his bike by a church in Peoria that had a neon sign that said, "Jesus Saves." This was during World War II, when people were saving everything—including gasoline, tin foil, and string. Wimber wondered "What does Jesus save?" He couldn't know what the church sign meant, because he didn't know he was lost and needed saving.

To communicate what it means to be lost and saved is one of the most difficult things to do in witnessing to another person in the American culture. In a survey of the beliefs of the people of the State of Minnesota, 51% said that they were not sinful. Today we buy perfume labeled "My Sin," and people half smile when they say, "I have sinned." Psychiatrist Dr. Karl Menninger wrote a book entitled *Whatever Became of Sin?* to call attention to the seriousness of not taking sin seriously.[1] The most sinister gangster who ever shot up Chicago, Al Capone, once said, "I have spent the best years of my life giving people the lighter pleasures, helping them have a good time, and all I get is abuse, the existence of a hunted man." He did not think that his stealing, robbing, and even killing made him a sinner. He thought of himself as a benefactor, unappreciated and misunderstood.

The first step in being saved has been taken by God when He through Jesus Christ objectively reconciled the world to Himself (cf. 2 Cor. 5:19). In order to become subjectively reconciled to God, however, or be saved, I need to admit that I am lost. The Holy Spirit through the office of the Law convinces me that I am a lost and condemned sinner, destined to receive my just reward in hell. Then through the Gospel, the Spirit creates faith in me, whereby I lay hold of the divine promises of grace in the Gospel and believe that I am saved by the only way I can be saved—through Jesus Christ, who both kept the Law perfectly in my place and suffered and died to pay for my sins.

Yes, Jesus saves! He saves the lost from sin and death and hell. To communicate that to someone who doesn't understand that they are lost is to fail to communicate a good message because they didn't first understand the bad message. In some churches this is spoken of as a Law and Gospel message. Before a person can understand or appreciate the Gospel, he must have heard the Law. The Law convicts of sin and the Gospel leads to the faith that receives the forgiveness of sins. I must know that I am lost before I can be saved! The goal of my witness to others is that I can be the means by which the Spirit of God leads a person to know that he is lost and then to find salvation in Jesus Christ. As the mission of Jesus was to seek and save the lost, so our mission is to do the same.

The Goal of Witness Is to Save

When I witness to my neighbor I may have different immediate goals, depending on the person and the situation. As I witness to John, my immediate goal may be to get him to attend church with me. When I witness to Jan I may want to help her find comfort in God's love to deal with a particular problem. When I witness to George I may want to lead him to see that there really is a God who made this world. These are all goals—immediate, short-range goals. The long-range or ultimate goal in all my witnessing, however, is the goal that Jesus gave me. As He came to seek and save the lost, so He has sent me to seek and save the lost. My goal is to save the lost, to have the lost come to faith in Jesus Christ, be born again, and become growing disciples of Jesus Christ.

In what has come to be known as the Great Commission, Jesus used different words than "save the lost" to describe the same thing when he said:

All authority in heaven and on earth has been given to
Me. Go therefore and make disciples of all nations, baptizing them in the name of the Father and of the Son
and the Holy Spirit, teaching them to observe all that
I have commanded you; and lo, I am with you always,
to the close of the age. (Matt. 28:18–20)

In that Great Commission there are four action verbs: go, make disciples, baptize, and teach. Only one of those verbs is an imperative, a command: "Make disciples." The other three verbs are supporting participles. Jesus said, as you go into the world, *I command you to make disciples* by baptizing and by teaching. The word for "make disciples," *mathēteuō*, as it is used in the

New Testament, sometimes means the same as it did among the Greeks, who used the word often. It means to follow the teachings of a great teacher, e.g., Socrates. In the New Testament there are disciples of the Pharisees, disciples of Moses, and disciples of John the Baptist. But when Jesus used the word and it came to be applied to those who followed His teaching, a new dimension was added. Jesus chose His disciples; they did not choose to follow Him. And when He chose them, they came into a personal relationship with Him. In that relationship they sought to become more and more like Him. The Great Commission mandates that disciples make disciples, Christians are to reproduce themselves.

The Holy Spirit is the only one who creates faith, but we are the instruments by which God brings to other people the Gospel, through which the Holy Spirit works that faith. Sometimes the New Testament puts the emphasis on proclaiming the Gospel message while at other times the emphasis is on the result, namely being saved or becoming disciples. When St. Paul spoke with the elders (pastors) of the large church at Ephesus, he said, "I reckon my own life to be worth nothing to me; I only want to complete my mission and finish the work that the Lord Jesus gave me to do, which is to declare the Good News about the grace of God" (Acts 20:24 TEV). Paul here spoke of his mission as preaching the Gospel, which is the means to accomplish the goal of saving. At other times Paul stresses the goal of saving more than the preaching. He says when speaking of his fellow Israelites, "My heart's desire and prayer to God for them is that they may be saved" (Rom. 10:1). In writing to the Corinthians, Paul insists that although he is a free man he is willing to be a slave in order to "win the more." He is willing to become a Jew to win Jews; to be under the Law to win those under the Law; to be weak to win those who are weak. Then he concludes, "I have become all things to all men, that I might by all means save some" (1 Cor. 9:19–22).

In his book, *Sharpening the Focus of the Church*, Gene A. Getz examines Greek words in the book of Acts that are used for what he called "evangelistic communication."[2] These are words that speak of communicating the Gospel message. Getz demonstrates that in each case the use of the word was not just to speak the Gospel but to achieve a goal or a purpose. The *purpose* of speaking a certain word was to evangelize, to have people believe the Gospel and come to be disciples of Jesus Christ. The *results* were not that everyone believed. When Paul preached at the Areopagus in Athens some mocked him, others put him off, and only a few believed (Acts 17:32–34).

Greek	English	Reference in Acts	Results
1. *laleō*	to speak	4:1	4:4—"many . . . believed"
2. *euange-lizō*	to speak good news	8:4	8:26—"the multitudes . . . gave heed"
3. *didaskō*	to teach	4:2	4:4—"many . . . who heard the word believed"
4. *kērussō*	to proclaim	8:5–6	8:12—"believed . . . were baptized"
5. *katag-gellō*	to announce	17:3	17:4—"some . . . were persuaded"
6. *diamar-turomai*	to bear witness	2:40	2:41—"were baptized"
7. *dialego-mai*	to reason, argue	18:4	18:8—"believed . . . were baptized"

One could add other New Testament words or derivatives of the above words that refer to communicating by teaching, to preaching, or to conversing with another person. But these seven words are the words that Getz holds up as the ones that are used of "evangelistic communication." These words are used to speak of communicating the message of the Gospel for the purpose of evangelizing, of saving people who would become disciples of Jesus Christ. He wants to point out that there was always a goal in the witnessing, the goal of having people believe, be baptized, and be saved.

The task of the church toward unbelievers is to preach the Gospel to them, proclaim salvation, and offer forgiveness. The results of the proclamation then are left to the Holy Spirit. While only God has the power to make the seed grow, the sower is concerned about whether the seed does grow or not. To sow and not look for a harvest is irresponsible farming. The witness of Jesus Christ witnesses with the ultimate goal in mind that the people to whom he witnesses will be saved, and become disciples of Jesus Christ. The command in the Great Commission is to "make disciples."

C. Peter Wagner emphasizes the goal of salvation with his definition of evangelism. Wagner is a professor of church growth at the School of World Mission at Fuller Theological Seminary, Pasadena, California. He, perhaps more than anyone else, has applied to American church life the church growth principles developed by Donald McGavran in the foreign mission fields. Wagner defines evangelism with three P's: Presence, Proclamation, and Persuasion. By "Persuasion" he means that the witness speaks the Gospel with the intent and purpose of having that person believe it and become a disciple of Jesus Christ. The word *persuade* is the Greek New Testament word *peithō* as used in such places in Acts as 13:43; 17:4; 18:4; 26:28; and 28:23–24 and translated in the Revised Standard Version by "urge" (Acts 13:43), "persuade" (Acts 17:4), and "convince" (Acts 28:23–24). This is the spirit in which the witness witnesses according to the example of the New Testament.

This difference between emphasizing the preaching of the Gospel or the result of the preaching, that of being saved, is highlighted in some of the official definitions of evangelism. A historic definition of evangelism, adopted by the Madras Foreign Mission Council, reads:

Evangelism is to present Jesus Christ to the world in the power of the Holy Spirit that men shall come to put their trust in God through Him as their Savior and serve Him as their Lord in the fellowship of His church.[3]

Some mission scholars have objected to the words "shall come" and would prefer "may come." After debating that issue, the Congress on World Evangelization in Lausanne, Switzerland, in 1974 framed this definition of evangelism and published it in the Lausanne Covenant: "Our Christian presence in the world is indispensable to evangelism, and so is that kind of dialog whose purpose it is to listen sensitively in order to understand. But evangelism itself is the proclamation of the historical, Biblical Christ as Savior and Lord, with a view to persuading people to come to him personally and so be reconciled to God."[4] In the section on "Comparing Methods" we will discuss *how* to ask for the response to the proclamation.

To sum up, as witnesses for Jesus Christ, we are to speak

the Gospel to people in order that they may repent and come to faith in Him, be baptized, and become a part of the church, His body. Mark said Jesus "went out and preached that men should repent" (Mark 6:12). Today every baptized Christian is the witness who is to "preach" that people repent, that is, be saved and become disciples of Jesus Christ.

In the days of the early settlement of the West, a territorial governor decided to give a pardon to a prisoner on death row, but he wanted to do it his own way. So he went to the prison and made the arrangements with the warden. Then he dressed as a clergyman and went alone to see the prisoner. When the prisoner saw him coming, he of course thought he was a clergyman and yelled, "Get away from me. I don't want to talk to you." The governor wouldn't give up easily. He pleaded with the prisoner. "I have something very important to offer to you, please listen to me." But the prisoner refused to listen to a word this "clergyman" had to say.

So the governor left. A short while later the warden came by, not knowing that the plan had failed. "Well, I guess you got your pardon," he cheerfully said. "What!" the shocked prisoner responded.

When the prisoner was executed as scheduled, he said to the warden as his last words: "Tell the world that I died not just because of my crimes, but because I would not listen to the pardon the governor wanted to give me." Jesus Christ has won a pardon for every one. He has "reconciled the world" (cf. 2 Cor. 5:19). It is our privilege, we who have received the pardon, to be bearers of the pardon to others. And the others are the prisoners on death row. Everyone who is not saved is lost! There is no middle ground.

The Holy Spirit Saves

As my Lord came to seek and to save the lost and as He has saved me, so now I am the one who is sent. I am to be seeking others who are lost, just as my Lord did. The difference, however, is how they are saved. I do not save them. I only find them and point them to the Savior, the same one who saved me. I cannot save anyone, and no one can save himself. St. Paul put it this way: "No one can say 'Jesus is Lord' but by the Holy Spirit" (1 Cor. 12:3).

It is true that sometimes the Bible speaks as if I can save

someone. St. Paul even said, "I have become all things to all men, that I might . . . save some" (1 Cor. 9:22). Jesus urged people, it seems, to save themselves. "Repent, and believe in the gospel" (Mark 1:15), and Peter commanded, "Repent, and be baptized" (Acts 2:38). Paul said to the jailer at Philippi, "Believe in the Lord Jesus Christ, and you will be saved" (Acts 16:31).

So while the Bible sometimes speaks as if one can save himself or that I can save someone, at other times it emphasizes strongly that no one can come to the Father unless, as Jesus said, the Father "draws him" (John 6:44). It is the Holy Spirit alone who creates faith when He enters the heart. Without the Spirit it is impossible to believe. "Whoever does not have the Spirit cannot receive the gifts that come from God's Spirit. Such a person really does not understand them; they are nonsense to him" (1 Cor. 2:14 TEV).

Some theologians suggest that Scripture speaks of conversion in a "double sense."[5] Jesus says, "Repent, and believe in the gospel" (Mark 1:15), and "No one can come to Me unless the Father who sent Me draws him" (John 6:44). The great Reformer, Martin Luther, suggests that to command men to believe or repent does not imply the ability to do so just as to command men to keep the commandments does not imply the ability to keep them. These "evangelical imperatives," as some call them, "repent" and "believe," rather than being an appeal to the human will as if it had the capability of converting itself, point rather to the "earnest desire of God for man's salvation and the urgent necessity of repentance."[6] He wrote, "I believe that I cannot by my own reason or strength believe in Jesus Christ, my Lord, or come to Him; but the Holy Ghost has called me by the Gospel, enlightened me with His gifts, sanctified and kept me in the true faith."[7] The Lutheran reformers put it this way in the Formula of Concord, Solid Declaration, II 7: "We believe that in spiritual and divine things the intellect, heart, and will of unregenerated man cannot by any native or natural powers in any way understand, believe, accept, imagine, will, begin, accomplish, do, effect, or cooperate, but that man is entirely and completely dead and corrupted as far as anything good is concerned."[8]

This is a mystery, a paradox that we accept. It is clear that although God converts, man does have the power to resist or to say no. Stephen charges the Jews with always resisting the Holy Spirit (cf. Acts 7:51). When He wept over the city of Jerusalem,

Jesus said that He sought to gather its people to Himself as a hen gathers her chicks but they "would not" (Matt. 23:37). Sometimes the Scripture speaks of man in his sin as being spiritually dead (Eph. 2:1) to emphasize his inability to believe or to respond to an invitation to believe the Gospel. Jesus said, "That which is born of the flesh is flesh, and that which is born of the Spirit is spirit" to emphasize that "unless one is born of water and the Spirit, he cannot enter the kingdom of God" (John 3:5–6).

Here is an analogy. I am lost in the woods and cannot find my way out. A rescue party comes in to find me. They offer to lead me to safety if I will follow them. Otherwise, if I refuse, I will wander around in the woods until I die. If I follow and am saved, the rescue party gets the credit for saving me. If I am lost, it is my own fault. There is one problem with that analogy. It seems as if I have the choice to say yes or to say no. Scripture says that I can say no, but that I cannot say yes until the Holy Spirit enters my heart and creates new life or the ability to say yes. When the Spirit does His work, then I am born again, then I cooperate with the Spirit as He continues to work in my life.

The explanation of the Third Article of the Apostles' Creed in Martin Luther's *Small Catechism* says it clearly: "I believe that I cannot by my own reason or strength believe in Jesus Christ, my Lord, or come to Him; but the Holy Ghost has called me by the Gospel, enlightened me with His gifts, sanctified and kept me in the true faith." This teaching is called monergism in contrast to the teaching which says that man is involved in the decision for his own salvation and which is called synergism, from the Greek words *syn* (with) and *ergon* (work).

The Means the Spirit Uses Is the Gospel

How does this Scriptural emphasis on monergism affect the way I witness to another person and seek a response from that person? The first thing that monergism emphasizes is that I must communicate the Gospel message, which is the means by which the Spirit calls people to faith and creates new life in them. St. Paul emphasized, "I am not ashamed of the gospel: it is the power of God for salvation to every one who has faith" (Rom. 1:16). The Greek word that Paul uses for "power" in the phrase, "power of God for salvation" is *dynamis*, the word from which we get our English word *dynamite*. The Gospel is the dynamite of God by which He destroys the old sinful nature in man and creates a new one.

Other passages in the Scripture speak of the same power of God in the "Word," the "cross," and the "preaching of Christ."

Is. 55:10–11: As the rain and the snow come down from heaven, and return not thither but water the earth, making it bring forth and sprout . . . so shall My word be that goes forth from My mouth; it shall not return to Me empty, but it shall accomplish that which I purpose, and prosper in the thing for which I sent it.

Rom. 10:17: Faith comes from what is heard, and what is heard comes by the preaching of Christ.

1 Cor. 1:18: The word of the cross is folly to those who are perishing, but to us who are being saved it is the power of God.

Acts 4:4 Many of those who heard the word believed.

The Word that God speaks saves. The Gospel message of the life, death, and resurrection of His Son is the power that changes people from being lost to being saved. This suggests that if I am to be involved in saving people, my involvement is in communicating the Gospel. A Boston physician explained it this way: "I cannot heal anyone. Only God can do that. The best I can do is to put a man under the most favorable conditions for God to heal him."[9]

In a series of articles on witnessing, Arthur Vincent says that the tragedy for Rip Van Winkle, the mountaineer in American folklore, was not that he slept for 20 years in the mountains, nor even that he slept through the Revolutionary War. The tragedy was that his musket was loaded and he didn't fire it![10] Our musket is loaded when we know the Gospel of Jesus Christ. It is a tragedy when we don't fire it, when we don't share the Gospel with the lost that they might be saved.

Comparing Methods

When Jesus began His ministry, He preached: "Repent, and believe in the gospel" (Mark 1:15). The Bible word for repentance is *metanoeō*, which means to have another mind, to change one's being. The word occurs 31 times in the New Testament. John the Baptist preached a "baptism of repentance" (Mark 1:4). Jesus commanded: When your brother says, "I repent," you must forgive him (Luke 17:4). To Peter He said, "When you have turned again [repented] strengthen your brethren" (Luke 22:32). After Easter, Jesus said that repentance and forgiveness of sins should be preached in His name to all nations (Luke 24:47). On Pentecost, Peter told the crowd, "Repent, and be baptized" (Acts 2:38).

Many methods of witnessing, especially as they are outlined in witnessing booklets like *The Four Spiritual Laws* of Campus Crusade and *Do You Know the Steps of Peace with God?* of the Billy Graham Evangelistic Association, point to man's sin and separation from God.

They stress the need to repent in words like these: "Man is sinful and separated from God." The witness needs to speak of sin and repentance in witnessing, but it is necessary first to determine by conversation where the person is spiritually. This means that the witness must keep clear the distinction between Law and Gospel. The Law shows one's sins; the Gospel points to the Savior from sin. The Law judges and condemns; the Gospel speaks forgiveness and comfort. The Law leads to repentance; the Gospel leads to new life. A person may be at different stages of understanding of sin and repentance and the need for the Gospel. The witness determines this with the Q-L-T method, (Question-Listen-Tell). The witness then speaks Law until he senses that the person is ready to hear the Gospel.

After presenting the Law and Gospel message, the witness then seeks a response to the message. In his evangelism workshops, Bob Scudieri builds a method of witness around the words: Care, Share, Dare. The Dare section stresses the need to "dare" to seek a response to the message. We believe that God's Spirit works through the Law-Gospel message, so we dare to ask what He has done. The witness booklets mentioned above stress the response as a decision that the person must make.

Elmer Kettner in *Adventures in Evangelism,* instead of speaking of a "decision" or "response," suggests the need to "create a desire" for the Gospel. He tells of a sales manager who said to him, "Salesmen and churchmen both fall down on Point 4." When asked what Point 4 was, he went on "In sales language it's asking for the order."[11]

"You mean we should press for a decision?" Kettner asked. "You know that the Gospel is free and received only as a gift

93

when the Holy Spirit creates faith. Aren't we helpless to decide until the Holy Spirit moves in?"

"Undoubtedly!" The salesman quickly responded. "But don't blame the Holy Spirit for your failure to use Point 4. Remember Elijah? He used it. He said, 'How long halt ye between two opinions? If the Lord be God, follow Him; but if Baal, then follow him.' . . . The prospect will not commit himself unless you invite him to do so."[12]

There is a proper way to use Point 4. When we witness to our neighbor, we can invite him to respond. The witnessing booklets mentioned above use words like, "Receive Jesus Christ as Savior and Lord by personal invitation," "Ask Jesus Christ to come into your life," or "Make a decision to accept Christ." The Evangelism Explosion method of D. James Kennedy speaks of asking people to make a "commitment" and suggests that a person in prayer "accept" Jesus as personal Savior and "receive" Him as Lord and Master.[13] These methods of witnessing are often based on the belief that man can make that decision himself or that he can at least cooperate with the Holy Spirit.

Two passages are usually cited for this method of inviting a response from the witness, John 1:12 and Rev. 3:20. John 1:12 reads: "To all who received him, who believed in His name, He gave power to become the children of God." The context of that verse is that the writer John was explaining that although Jesus came into the world as the true Light, His own chosen people, the Jews at Nazareth, His own home, did not accept Him as such. But everyone who did accept Him as the Light, or as the Messiah, they were by the power of God born into a relationship where they could be called the Sons of God. The word "receive" has the meaning of believe, and there is no emphasis on inviting Jesus into your life.

Rev. 3:20 reads: "Behold, I stand at the door and knock; if any one hears My voice and opens the door, I will come in to him and eat with him, and he with Me." These words are addressed to a Christian congregation, the one in Laodicea, which was "lukewarm" (3:15–16). Jesus is calling the congregation to repent and renew their zeal. The one who "hears my voice" receives new life and is able to open the door. He has been born again by the Gospel, and with the power of the Spirit of God in him, he is able now to cooperate in his growth in faith. Jesus coming in is not to create faith but to strengthen faith. So theologians speak of this passage as referring to sanctification rather than justification. It is the Christian opening the door to greater fellowship with Christ.

So what sort of response should I ask for when I witness? If I am talking about salvation or explaining the Gospel, I may simply ask, "Have I made myself clear?" "Does that make sense to you?" "Do you believe that?" Biesenthal in *Dialog Evangelism* suggests that we must be sensitive to what the Holy spirit is doing in the heart of the hearer through the Gospel. The person must be led to acknowledge what the Holy Spirit has done and encouraged to go on from there.[14] The responses I may ask for are: "Will you read this tract?" "Will you read the Gospel of John?" "Will you come to church with me?" "Will you pray with me?"

One lady talked to her neighbor about coming to church with her. She complained, "I have invited her to church five times! What should I do?" The neighbor wasn't ready for that kind of response. This was as someone suggested, "tugging at green fruit." She needed more of the Word of God and the power of the Spirit. She felt no need to go to church. No desire was created. In this case, when there is a rejection of the first choice of response, I seek a second option, which may be merely to keep the channels of communication open so that I can witness again at another time. And then I keep trying to create the desire for forgiveness and peace and a relationship with the church. Often that desire is best created through my own personal testimony. It is *not* achieved through debate or argument. Richard Korthals in his book *Agape Evangelism* emphasizes throughout that people are loved into the Kingdom, not argued into it.[15]

S is for Saved. As Jesus came to save, so I am sent to save. It is the Holy Spirit who actually saves, but He works through the Gospel, which I present in my witness. I tell my story, listen to the prospect's story, and relate our stories to His story. As my conversation revolves around the three stories, using the Q-L-T method (Question-Listen-Tell), I speak the Gospel, which is the power of God for salvation (Rom. 1:16). The Holy Spirit creates new life. But not everyone to whom I witness is saved. The Holy Spirit in His own time calls those who are chosen to be saved. Some resist the Holy Spirit and so will never be saved. That is the subject of the next chapter.

For Further Study and Action

1. Read the entire section in which St. Paul speaks about "saving some," 1 Cor. 9:21–23. List the four groups of people that he wants to "win." Is there a difference between "win" and "save?"

2. This chapter emphasized that every disciple is a witness. Another emphasis could have been that the disciples witness to everyone, to those of all ages and cultures and of every social and economic status. God loved "the world"; Christ reconciled "the world." Can you recall any passages that speak of witnessing to everyone?

3. Some examples of conversions recorded in the book of Acts show how people were saved. They do not all follow the same pattern. Each is a separate and distinct case. Read the following accounts and draw some conclusions. It is helpful to put the following Bible stories and topics on an 8½-by-11-inch sheet of paper and write a few key words in the blanks.

4. We have said in this chapter that people must repent of past sins before they can believe the Gospel. Is there a difference between showing a person the sins of his life and "creating a desire" for the Gospel? How do you understand the related term of "creating a felt need" for the Gospel? Read John 8:1–11. Why didn't Jesus speak to the woman caught in adultery about her sin?

5. Do you know of people who are lost, who will go to hell because they have not accepted the pardon available to them through Jesus Christ? Pray for them and try to find ways in which they might be saved! If in a group, share your experiences with them.

6. Robert Preus tells of a teacher who likened conversion to an operation on a very sick man. The doctor assured the patient that he could save him, but the man had to give his assent before the operation could be performed. Can man assent to this conversion? Is man sick in sin or dead in sin? Is this an illustration of justification or sanctification? Preus said, "In conversion God alone is active, giving us a new life."[16]

	Eunuch of Ethiopia Acts 8:4–13, 26–40	Saul of Tarsus Acts 9:1–22	Cornelius of Caesarea Acts 10:1–45	Lydia of Philippi Acts 16:11–15	Jailer of Philippi Acts 16:19–34
God's Initiative					
Creating Desire					
Gospel Presented					
Baptism					
Holy Spirit					
Result					

7. S for Some _____

Seven-year-old Michael was rushed to Lutheran Hospital in St. Louis with a burst appendix. His roommate in the hospital was a senior student from Concordia Seminary in St. Louis. As they became acquainted, the student discovered that neither Michael nor his parents went to any church, even though his father was reared in the Roman Catholic Church and his mother had Methodist roots. So he witnessed to them about his faith in Jesus Christ and encouraged the parents to enroll Michael in a Lutheran elementary school. After 23 days Michael was released from the hospital, but he and his parents remembered that seminary student and his witness to them. So, they sought out Trinity Lutheran School in south St. Louis and enrolled Michael. Michael brought home his Bible history books, his catechism, and many invitations to worship at Trinity Lutheran Church. Soon the mother took instructions and joined the church and the father followed.

During his high-school years Michael met another student from Concordia Seminary and this time the student urged him to study for the ministry. Michael laughed—but after thinking and talking more about it, he did enroll in a preparatory school. That was the first step that led him to become a Lutheran pastor. Later he became the president of one of the largest colleges of The Lutheran Church—Missouri Synod and then became an executive leader of the church's international offices.[1]

What an unusual story! Unusual because we seldom see the results of our witness, and here is a case of very dramatic results! Unusual because three people were saved, and few of the many to whom we witness are saved. Unusual because of the many, many years that were involved in the result of two simple witnesses, a student in a hospital and a student working with high-school kids.

One *S* in our acrostic on the word *Witness* can help us think of those who are saved, as we did in the last chapter. The second *S* in *Witness* can remind us that only some are saved. S is for

Some. That is the message of this chapter.

The Response to Witness Varies

When I witness to Jesus Christ, I never know what the response or the final results will be. That doesn't affect my witnessing. I witness, whether or not I see results. I witness regardless of what the response may be. The response may be indifference, rejection, objection, or acceptance. Let's examine each of these a little more closely.

When I reflect my faith in my daily conversation and say to a friend, "May God bless your day!" there may be no response at all, or an indifferent shrug or look. When I invite a friend to attend a church function with me, there may be a simple "I'm busy, maybe some other time." When I talk to a friend repeatedly over a long period of time about Jesus Christ, he may put up with my witness and let me talk when I want to because he is a friend, but it means nothing to him. He shrugs it off with an indifferent attitude of toleration. I must learn to expect that this will often be the response to my witness.

When the Gallup Poll asks people about their church affiliation, it indicates that 6–7%, or about 10–12 million, of the adult population (18 or older) in the United States claim no religious preference. However, when the pollsters ask how many are affiliated with a church, the figures jump to 40%, or 61 million, who are unchurched.[2] When, however, churches total their church membership statistics they come up with 50% of the adult population who are churched, or 85 million who are unchurched.[3] In other words, by even the most conservative estimate, 40–50% of the adult population is unchurched—60 to 80 million Americans 18 or over. These people do not attend or participate in a church or synagogue by worship or other activities. Many of them have not rejected their faith by a conscious decision but are indifferent to it and its expectations. Some of the people to whom we witness will be these kinds of people, people who have already adopted a life-style that is based on indifference to religion. Their first response to your witness will probably also be indifference. We must expect this and in patience and love try to develop the kind of relationship that allows us to continue to witness. We hope and pray that some day the Spirit of God will be able to reach them and create a desire for the Gospel and a felt need for the church.

At other times the response to our witness will be outright rejection. I was wearing a Jesus pin as I took my seat on an airplane next to a man with jeans and long hair. "What does your pin say," he asked, as many people do when they see the word Jesus in reverse computer style letters. I gave him my card and said in my usual style, "The same thing my card says." He studied it until the word became clear to him and then he said, "What's he running for?" (It was during campaign season for the national elections.) He let me know by his tone of voice and his attitude that he wasn't about to listen to any talk from me about Jesus. He rejected my witness even before I gave it.

Most of the 60 to 80 million unchurched adults in the United States claim to believe in God, and many claim to believe that Jesus Christ is God's Son. Surprisingly, most of them have been associated at one time with a church. That is, they were members of a church at one time in their lives, or were at least brought up in a church. They left the church. They rejected the witness of the church and the Christians in the church. Why?

Why did they leave the church, and why are they unchurched? The answers they give are diverse. John O'Hara summarized some of the findings of the researchers in this way:

● Very few left the church for doctrinal reasons.

● A significant minority may have left due to interpersonal conflict with either the pastor or another member.

● The largest group left for reasons of personal convenience, family reasons, or life-style reasons—they married someone of a different faith, moved, had a change in work schedule, etc. There is a significant degree of social distance between the churched and the unchurched. The latter have very few friends who are active church members. If married, their spouse tends to be inactive as well. To a large extent "churched" and "unchurched" describes two distinctive subcultures in U.S. society.[4]

When we witness to the unchurched, we need to understand the social distance that may exist between us and the underlying "values gap" that produces it. Because of this, the initial response to our witness to Jesus and the Gospel, as well as to the church, may be one of rejection. The unchurched have already rejected the church and commitment to Jesus Christ in favor of their own life-style, which focuses on personal satisfaction and pleasure.

When we witness to them, we should be ready to accept

rejection. But that doesn't stop our witness. It should make us more determined to find a way to reach that person, to understand why they rejected the church and gently continue to witness to them.

Other responses to our witness might be some specific objections:

"The church is full of hypocrites."

"I can be as good a Christian as any of you in church."

"All the church wants is my money."

"I can handle things by myself; I don't need the church to lean on."

Some writers who seek to provide help in dealing with objections in witnessing point out that some objections are real or sincere obstacles to the person who speaks them, while other are merely alibis or excuses. In any case, they must be dealt with. Donald Abdon suggested what he considered a "simple, four-step" method for managing the objection so that the witness to the real subject, the Gospel, can be discussed.[5]

Step 1: Determine the Real Objection
Step 2: Accept the Objection
Step 3: Reassert the Subject
Step 4: Reaffirm the Gospel

Abdon then lists 40 objections, divides them into 7 specific categories and demonstrates under each of the categories how to apply the four-step method. His categories are:

1. Substitutes for Christ
2. Self-Righteousness
3. Blaming Other People
4. The Organized Church
5. "Intellectual" Difficulties
6. The Environment
7. Life Itself.

Here is a demonstration of dealing with several of the objections, using especially steps 2, 3, and 4. Step 1: "Determine the real objection" is often a matter of longer discussion and the development of trust.

Objection: "All religions are the same."

Step 2 (Accept the Objection): "I know that there are a lot of people who think that there are certain similarities in religions."

Step 3 (Reassert the Subject): "But there is one basic difference. A religion is something people *do* or *practice*. Christianity isn't a religion; it's a *faith.*"

Step 4 (Reaffirm the Gospel): "Christ is the center of that faith. To be a Christian is to know and believe in a Person—Jesus Christ."

Objection: "I'll straighten out my life first, then I'll come to church."

Step 2: "You know, there are a lot of people who think that. But that is like saying that I'm sick, so I'll wait till I get well and then go to see the doctor."

Step 3: "Only God can straighten out our life so that it is really good for us and pleasing to Him."

Step 4: "That's why God sent His Son Jesus Christ for us."

Objection: "I don't have to go to church to be a Christian."

Step 2: "You are absolutely right. Nowhere does the Bible command us to 'go' to church." Other comments might be: "Perhaps you are defining the word 'Christian' differently than I do. I would like to share with you what 'Christian' means to me." Or "I believe that God assumes Christians don't have to be *told* to go to church."

Step 3: "What God talks about is *worship*, which means to place a value or declare the worth. Christians gather to worship because they want to tell each other and the world about the value they place on God. He is first in their lives."

Step 4: "St. Paul once said, 'You are bought with a price.' The price was the lifeblood of the Son of God, Jesus Christ. That's how much value God places on us."

The final response and the best, of course, is that people hear the Gospel and are saved. The Christian witness rejoices when he is permitted to see this happen, but he conditions himself to keep witnessing, even though he doesn't see it happen. Sometimes the response takes years. Church Growth scholars suggest that a person on the average hears the Gospel seven different times before he makes a response to it. But some are really saved. That is the promise of our Lord when we witness because the Gospel is the "power of God for salvation" (Rom. 1:16). His Word will not return void; it will accomplish what He pleases (cf. Is. 55:10–11). As a Christian witness we do seek a response and pray for results, but we learn to expect different kinds of responses: indifference, rejection, and objections. Some will be saved, but we leave that in the hands of our Lord. While we do seek a response our primarily responsibility is to speak the Gospel faithfully and apply it so that the power of God can work.

A Christian man sought to witness to his seating partner on the plane. The man, however, responded by letting the witness know that he didn't want to hear any of his God-talk. So the Christian witness remained silent. Soon the plane went through some rough weather. After the plane bounced a few times, the seating partner turned to the Christian witness and snidely suggested, "Can't you talk to the man upstairs and do something about this weather?" The Christian witness thought for a moment and then said, "Well, sir, it's like this. The weather is the business of the management. I'm only in the sales department."

God is the one who saves, even though people have the power to resist the work of His Spirit. Our task in the *sales department* is to share the products, to tell others about the Gospel of Jesus Christ, the free forgiveness and eternal life offered to all. We want them to believe it and be saved, but since we can't force them, we leave that in the *hands of the management*, the Almighty God.

I Make My Witness Winsome

That's not easy! It's not easy to continue to witness, even though I see no results. It's not easy for a farmer to continue to plow the ground, sow his seed, cultivate, and see little harvest. The only way that I can continue to witness in hope and enthusiasm is to see myself as part of a team. St. Paul in writing to his congregation at Corinth says, "I planted [the seed in the Word], Apollos watered, but God gave the growth." He then points out "Neither he who plants nor he who waters is anything, but only God who gives the growth. He who plants and he who waters are equal, and each shall receive his wages according to his labor. For we are God's fellow workers" (1 Cor. 3:5–9). I am part of a team, one of the servants through whom God gives the growth. I may sow and water, but I may or may not see the harvest.

The reason that I continue to sow or to water is my relationship to Christ, not the results that I see. Peter uses the phrase, "reverence Christ as Lord" in your hearts (1 Peter 3:15). It is because Christ is in my heart that I can keep on witnessing to Him. Peter says that wives married to unbelieving husbands should continue to seek to save them, though their witness may be rejected or ignored. They should keep on living their Christian lives, submissive to their husbands in the prayer and hope that they may be won without a word because of their lives, when they see their reverent and chaste behavior (cf. 1 Peter 3:1–2). In this spirit of reverence to Christ as Lord, the Christian is, as Peter says, always to be prepared to make a defense to anyone who calls them to account for the hope that is in them (cf. 1 Peter 3:15). He is speaking about those who must suffer for their faith, for those who suffer without just cause. The Christian witness continues to give his witness, to explain to others why he is "zealous for what is right" (1 Peter 3:13) and why he seeks to witness "with gentleness and reverence" (1 Peter 3:15).

Once I boarded a Trailways bus in St. Louis on my way to Troy, Illinois, where I lived at the time. The only seat left was at the very rear of the bus. I sat next to a rather shabbily dressed middle-aged man. As the bus began to move out of the station, my seating companion started talking, and we became acquainted. He was going to Vandalia to spend Christmas with his four-year-old son. He showed me pictures. I listened. I couldn't quite understand why he was living in St. Louis and his wife and son were in Vandalia. I asked, "What do you do in St. Louis for a living?" "I steal," he responded. I continued to ask questions. What do you mean? How long have you been stealing? I listened. He explained how he had been a boxer—and he showed me some pictures from his wallet. We hadn't talked long when he lifted the brown bag that he held between his feet, asked, "Mind if I have a drink?" and tilted his bottle for a snort. And he kept snorting off and on during our conversation.

I learned that his wife, a Lutheran, had left him. He had been Catholic but now insisted, "A man cannot forgive my sins." As we talked I remembered that passage from 1 Peter 3:15— give an answer for the hope in you—with *gentleness* and *reverence.* I could have told him it was a sin to steal and scolded him. I could have said, "Yes, I mind if you have a drink. Don't you know it is against the law to drink on a public bus. What are you—an alcoholic?" But I listened and when possible gave a simple witness. "Man cannot forgive, yes, but God can." He said, "The church doesn't understand. You preachers don't know what it is like to be an alcoholic." I didn't argue.

When it was time for me to leave the bus, after 45 minutes of conversation with my new-found friend, he promised me that

104

he would take his four-year-old son to church on Christmas and that he would try to seek help for his drinking problem. I don't know the final results. I leave that to God and pray that others will continue to sow seeds and that some will water the seeds. I was thankful that I remembered the verse "with gentleness and reverence," because that allowed me to sow the seeds. And as I reflected on that experience I also remembered the words of St. Paul, "I have become all things to all men, that I might by all means save some" (1 Cor. 9:22). And I prayed for my former boxer-alcoholic-stealing friend.

I Pray for My Witness

When I teach people to go door-to-door making witness surveys or a simple canvass of a neighborhood, I suggest the simple "sidewalk prayer," a prayer that callers may speak in their hearts as they walk down the sidewalk, and even as they ring the door-bell:

O Holy Spirit, prepare the way,

And teach me Lord, just what to say.

After using this prayer for a number of years, it occurred to me to ask how Biblical this prayer really was. After all, it does not say anything about converting anyone, or bringing anyone to church. So I studied what the Scriptures say about praying for the work of evangelism and came up with the following eight points:

1. *I thank God for what He is already doing.*

When I begin to witness to a person, I don't know how many other people have witnessed before me, nor what God is already doing in the heart of that person. After the baptism of the 3,000 on the day of Pentecost, "the Lord added to their number day by day those who were being saved" (Acts 2:47). I thank God for all those who are already saved and those whom God is continuing to save. He is already doing it even without my prayer.

2. *I ask God to help me want what He wants.*

When Jesus looked at the crowds that were coming to Him, He had compassion on them for they were "like sheep without a shepherd" (Matt. 9:36; Mark 6:34). He was moved. As the Son of God, He was on earth in order to bring them peace and new life. It was His will, as it was the will of His Father who sent Him, "that all should reach repentance" (2 Peter 3:9; cf. 1 Tim. 2:4). I learn to pray that His will be my will, that I desire the salvation of all the people in my extended family, in my neighborhood, and in my social and recreational contacts. That is not easy. Some of them are good people. Some of them are mean and evil. Some of them won't listen to me or will even ridicule me. Yet I ask God to give me the desire that they all be saved, and only when I want what God wants will I become serious in my witnessing to them.

3. *I pray that I will be what is necessary to win others.*

"You are the salt of the earth" (Matt. 5:13). I pray that my life will make people thirsty for the Water of life. "You are the light of the world" (Matt. 5:14). I pray that my light will so shine that, as Jesus said, people "may see your good works and give glory to your Father who is in heaven" (Matt. 5:16). My life is the light that leads men to glorify the Father. "Reverent and chaste behavior" wins the unbelieving (1 Peter 3:1–2).

But as I relate to specific individuals, I can learn from St. Paul, who sought to be all things to all men without compromising the Gospel. Paul went so far as to say that "I have made myself a slave to all, that I might win the more" (1 Cor. 9:19–22). When he was with Jews, he sought to live like a Jew, so as not to offend them as they kept their dietary laws and the ceremonies at the temple. When he was with those who were weak, he became like a weak person, yet without compromising his faith, just in order to win some of those who were weak. My prayer has to be that I will be what I ought to be in order that God's plan might be carried out and some come to faith.

4. *I pray for workers in the harvest.*

When Jesus saw the multitudes who were like sheep without a shepherd, who were harassed and helpless, He told His disciples, "The harvest is plentiful, but the laborers are few; pray therefore the Lord of the harvest to send out laborers into His harvest" (Matt. 9:36–38). The harvest is still plentiful but the problem still is that there are too few harvesters. So we are to "pray the Lord of the harvest to send out laborers into His harvest." This suggests that I, as a Christian witness, pray for professional church leaders, pastors, directors of evangelism, directors of Christian education, and all church workers that they might see part of their ministry as reaping and bringing in the harvest. I also ask God to help the lay members of the church see the multitudes who are "harassed and helpless" (Matt. 9:36) in our world and be just as concerned over them as Jesus was, and then be about the work of harvesting.

5. *I pray for opportunities to speak.*

St. Paul wrote to the congregation of Christians at Colossae, "Be persistent in prayer, and keep alert as you pray, giving thanks to God. At the same time pray also for us, so that God will give us a good opportunity to preach his message about the secret of Christ" (Col. 4:2–3 TEV). The "secret of Christ" was that He is the Savior of the Gentiles as well as the Jews. Paul said that the reason he was in prison was this, that he could have the opportunity to tell Gentiles about it. I also need to pray for opportunities, and especially for the attitude of St. Paul. God will arrange opportunities for me to witness wherever my daily duties take me. I need to learn to recognize the opportunities and use them when they come. Often there are opportunities all around me, and I don't recognize them.

The May 1940 cover of *Time* magazine featured Pastor Martin Niemöller of Germany. It carried the caption: "In Germany the cross has not bowed to the Swastika." The Nazis imprisoned Pastor Niemöller. The story is told that during his fourth year in prison he dreamed that Hitler was standing before the bar of judgment pleading with God that he had not heard the Gospel. In the dream Niemöller heard God's voice say to him, "Were you with him one whole hour and did not tell him about My Son?" When he awoke, Niemöller remembered that he had indeed spent an hour with Hitler and that he did not tell him. After that Niemöller began to witness to everyone he met—the guards, every visitor, anyone who would listen.

The people we meet every day are potential opportunities for witness!

6. *I pray for the right words to say.*

Paul was concerned that when he had his opportunity to witness, he might be able to speak words that people would understand: "Pray that I may speak, as I should, in such a way as to make it clear" (Col. 4:4 TEV). And he even suggests more in advising the Colossians to witness. "Your speech should always be pleasant and interesting, and you should know how to give the right answer to everyone" (Col. 4:6 TEV).

7. *I pray for boldness.*

Paul also asked the Christians in the congregation at Ephesus to pray for his witness and included in this instance the prayer to speak boldly, "Pray also for me, that God will give me a message when I am ready to speak, so that I may speak boldly and make known the gospel's secret" (Eph. 6:1 TEV).

An example of praying for boldness is recorded in Acts in what is sometimes called the story of the "second Pentecost." Peter and John were threatened by the Sanhedrin and told to stop preaching about Jesus. This was followed by a prayer meeting in which a group of Christians prayed about the threats. It is interesting that they did not pray that God would prevent persecution or harm, or that God would hinder the Jewish court from carrying out their threats. Instead they prayed, "Lord, look upon their threats, and grant to Thy servants to speak Thy word with all boldness" (Acts 4:29). "And when they had prayed, the place in which they were gathered together was shaken; and they were all filled with the Holy Spirit and spoke the word of God with boldness" (Acts 4:31).

8. *I pray for the Holy Spirit.*

Jesus promised that when His disciples received the Holy Spirit they would receive power to witness (Acts 1:8), and on Pentecost they were filled with the Holy Spirit and spoke "as the Spirit gave them utterance" (Acts 2:4). I too can pray for the special measure of the Holy Spirit in order that I can speak the Word with boldness, and God's promise is, "If you then, who are evil, know how to give good gifts to your children, how much more will the heavenly Father give the Holy Spirit to those who ask Him!" (Luke 11:13).

The shortest way to a person's heart is through the heart of God. Prayer is preparation for my witness. It prepares both me and the person to whom I witness. A simple, easy-to-remember prayer is:

Lord, lay some soul upon my heart,
And love that soul through me.
And may I gladly do my part,
To win that soul for Thee.

And then substitute the name of one person for the word *soul.*

Lord, lay _____ upon my heart,
And love _____ through me.
And may I gladly do my part,
To win _____ for Thee.

I Rejoice When Some Are Saved

Only some of those to whom we witness are saved. Only some of the lost are found. But when just one of them is found, we rejoice with thankful hearts. That is the message that our Savior spoke dramatically in the parables of Luke 15. He spoke them to the Pharisees who complained that He "receives sinners and eats with them" (Luke 15:2). In each parable—of the lost sheep, the lost coin, and the lost son—when the lost was found, there was rejoicing.

The shepherd has 100 sheep, but when one of them goes astray, he leaves the 99 and goes to search for the one that is lost. And when he finds it he puts it on his shoulders "rejoicing," calls together his friends and neighbors, saying to them, "Rejoice with me, for I have found my sheep which was lost." Then Jesus adds, "Just so, I tell you, there will be more joy in heaven over one sinner who repents than over ninety-nine righteous persons who need no repentance" (Luke 15:6–7).

After the woman finds her lost coin and rejoices with her friends and neighbors, Jesus adds, "there is joy before the angels of God over one sinner who repents" (Luke 15:10).

In the parable of the prodigal son, the father is so happy to see the son return that he runs to meet him, embraces him, kisses him over and over, and orders a big celebration with the fatted calf, with music and dancing, so that they can "make merry." And when the other son complains about all the fuss over the son who wasted his money on harlots, the father chides him by saying that it is fitting to make merry and be glad; "for this your brother was dead, and is alive; he was lost, and is found" (Luke 15:11–32). Someone has said, "The feast indicates the joy of a forgiving God over a forgiven man and the joy of a forgiven man over a forgiving God." If the angels in heaven rejoice over one sinner who repents, should not we in the church on earth rejoice?

A Christian lady in her commitment to her Lord came to the point where she could say, "Lord, I'm available. If you want me to witness today to someone at my door or even on the telephone, I'm ready." Ten minutes later the phone rang. To her surprise it was an obscene caller on the other end. Instead of hanging up, she listened to his lewd comments and the questions he asked. When he had had his say, she spoke up, "You've asked me some questions, now may I ask you something." "Sure, lady," the caller replied.

"It's obvious," she said, "that you are looking for some form of love, right?"

The surprised caller responded, "Well, you could say that, lady."

"Well, I can introduce you to someone who can love you in a way that you have never been loved before."

"Lady, what are you talking about?" The caller was puzzled but curious. The lady went on to explain her faith in the love of God, and the lewd phone caller finally said, "Lady, are there more people like you in this world?"

"Yes, there are. Down on the corner of 28th and Sheridan there is a whole church full of us." And she went on to make an appointment to meet him on Sunday morning before church in the lobby. He came. He went to church and came back—and back until he finally joined the church.[6]

This is an unusual example of one who was "lost and is found" but it does happen! It happens every day when, as Church Growth researchers like C. Peter Wagner[7] tell us, 78,000 new Christians are added every day to the 1.4 billion people in the Christian church on earth. Many of the new Christians are children born of Christian parents, but thousands upon thousands of them are adults who come to faith in Jesus Christ. How the angels in heaven must rejoice!

Sometimes it may be hard for us in the United States to rejoice because much of the growth of the church today is in other countries of the world, like Africa and Korea. Some denominations in the United States are growing, although many of them have reached a plateau in their growth line or are declining. But even in denominations that are gaining people for Christ, some members see few results in their own congregation or in their own witness. I need to see myself as one of the "friends and neighbors" in the parables of the lost who were found in Luke 15. Then I can join the "merrymaking" over the 78,000 that are found every day. When my congregation receives new members, I join the angels in heaven in rejoicing. And when by the grace of God I see some results in one person to whom I witness, I praise and thank God for this great and wonderful joy.

Even when I see no results, I can learn to rejoice at least that I had an opportunity to sow the seeds, or water and cultivate what others have sown. I see myself as part of God's team reaching out to touch and win the lost. My seating companion on one plane trip was a young professional-looking lady. As we became acquainted, I discovered through my questions that she was a research analyst working for the Federal government on her way to study the problems of the fishing industry in the State of Washington. She found out that I was a minister working for the church. I was following the usual procedure discussed earlier—Q-L-T (Question-Listen-Tell). I began to move from the chitchat to church, with the intention of moving the conversation to faith (chitchat-church-faith). I asked, "Do you have any church background?"

"Yes, I was raised as a Catholic. Even graduated from a Catholic high school."

"Are you still active in the Catholic Church?"

"No, I never go to church any more."

"Why? With all that training through high school . . . you gave it up?"

"Well, today I'm an atheist."

"What do you mean? Do you believe that this world just came about by itself without any divine guidance? And that today everything and everybody just operates and functions without a Supreme Being?"

"Why not? I see no need for a God."

This is how the Question and Listening went. Occasionally I inserted a Telling, which was a personal testimony, telling my story. "That doesn't satisfy me. I believe that an Almighty God in infinite wisdom designed and created the whole universe and today rules and controls it. But, tell me, what do you believe about life after death?"

She tried to tell me but she was uncertain. "Maybe there is some big soul out there beyond where we are all absorbed, or something. I don't think about that much. I have a lot of living to do right now."

"I can live better right now when I know that there is something better after this life, that a loving God has prepared a place where I will live with Him in all eternity."

So the conversation went for over an hour. When the plane arrived at our destination I thanked her for the conversation. She said, "I enjoyed talking to you. I guess I'll have to think about it some more." I did not see her saved or hear her make a promise

111

to return to her church. But I could rejoice in the opportunity to sow some seed. I saw a tiny "result" in her willingness to reconsider her "atheism," and I could rejoice in that. I could pray that someday the angels in heaven will rejoice to see her as one who was lost but was found.

Theodore Raedeke, executive director of Key 73, an interdenominational evangelism emphasis in the early 1970s, used to tell the story of John Broadus. Broadus became a Christian when he was a teenager. The very next day he shared his new faith with one of his schoolmates, Sandy Jones, a redheaded, awkward farm boy. "I wish you would be a Christian, too. Won't you?" he pleaded. Soon Sandy Jones did become a Christian. The first thing he did after he joined the church was to shake John's hand and say, "Thank you, John."

John Broadus grew up and became a clergyman and the president of a school where ministers and missionaries were trained. Every summer John would come back to his hometown for a visit. And every time the word got around that John Broadus was in town, the farmer in plain clothes, sometimes with mud on his shoes, would come, stick out his big hand and say, "Howdy, John. Thank you, John. I will never forget."

When John Broadus neared the end of this life, his family gathered around his sick bed. Sandy Jones had already died. John said, "The sweetest sound to my ears when I get to heaven, next to the welcome of Jesus, will be the welcome of Sandy Jones. He will thrust out his big hand and say, 'Howdy, John. Thank you, John.'"

Oh, give me, Lord, Thy love for souls,
For lost and wandering sheep.
That I may see the multitudes
And weep as Thou didst weep.

From off the altar of Thy heart
Take Thou some flaming coals,
Then touch my life and give me, Lord,
A heart that burns for souls.

When I enter that beautiful city,
And the saved all around me appear,
May I then hear somebody tell me,
It was you who invited me here.

For Further Study and Action

1. Read 1 Peter 3:1–6. How are the unbelieving won "without a word" (v. 1)? What is "reverent and chaste behavior" (v. 2)? What is a "gentle and quiet spirit" (v. 4)? Can a person come to faith without knowing the Gospel of Jesus Christ? Compare Rom. 10:17.
2. Read Matthew's account of the parable of the lost sheep, Matt. 18:10–14. Who are the "little ones" spoken of in verses 10 and 14? In Luke's account the angels rejoice when a lost one is found. Who is happy here?
3. Roleplay in a Bible study or witness class with another person to practice the Q-L-T method (Question-Listen-Tell).
4. Write out on cards a few Bible verses that contain the Gospel that could be used for your witness. Select from passages like John 3:16; John 14:6; Acts 2:38; Acts 4:12; Acts 16:31; Rom. 5:8–9; and Rom. 3:23 with 6:23.
5. Researchers have listed 43 life-changing events that they call a "Social readjustment rating scale." These are times when people are open to listening to a witness and are in need of our prayers. Below are 12 of the 43 life-changing events. Behind each write the name of a person you know who has gone through this experience in the last 12 months. Use this as your witness and prayer list. Change it regularly.
    1. Death of a spouse _____
    2. Divorce _____
    3. Marital separation _____
    4. Jail term _____
    5. Death of a close family member _____
    6. Personal injury or illness _____
    7. Marriage _____
    8. Fired at work _____
    9. Marital reconciliation _____
    10. Retirement _____
    11. Change in health of a family member _____
    12. Pregnancy _____

Notes

Introduction
1. Kenneth C. Haugk, *Christian Caregiving: A Way of Life* (Minneapolis: Augsburg Publishing House, 1984), pp. 11–12.

Chapter 1
1. *Evangelism and Social Responsibility: An Evangelical Commitment*, Lausanne Occasional Paper No. 21. Published jointly by the Lausanne Committee for World Evangelization and the World Evangelical Fellowship, 1982.
2. Milton L. Rudnick, *Speaking the Gospel Through the Ages: A History of Evangelism* (St. Louis: Concordia Publishing House, 1984), p. 68.
3. Richard Lischer, *Speaking of Jesus* (Philadelphia: Fortress Press, 1982), pp. 12–13.
4. Ibid., p. 17.
5. Haugk, p. 18.

Chapter 2
1. Merton P. Strommen, and others, *A Study of Generations* (Minneapolis: Augsburg Publishing House, 1972).
2. Ibid.
3. Delos Miles, *Overcoming Barriers to Witnessing* (Nashville: Broadman Press, 1984).
4. Paul J. Foust and Richard G. Korthals, *Reach Out: Evangelism for the Joy of It* (St. Louis: Concordia Publishing House, 1984), p. 29.
5. Ibid. p. 30.
6. Lischer, pp. 12–13.
7. Miles, p. 260.
8. This and four other Witness Word pins and cards are available from the Board for Evangelism Services, The Lutheran Church—Missouri Synod, 1333 S. Kirkwood Road, St. Louis, MO 63122. The other words are Love, Peace, Joy, Life, each in a different color. Other helps are available also from the same source.
9. Two such booklets are available from the Board for Evangelism Services (see note 8): "You Can Be Sure," which is organized around the Kennedy outline, and "A Personal Faith—Now and Forever," which is a simple outline of the Gospel message with Bible verses. Most denominations have booklets similar to these, such as "The Four Spiritual Laws" of Campus Crusade for Christ.
10. American Tract Society, Oradell, NJ 07649; Concordia Tract Mission, Box 201, St. Louis, MO 63166; Faith Prayer and Tract league, 934 11th St., NW, Grand Rapids, MI 49504; Good News Publishers, Westchester, IL.
11. Concordia Tract Mission, St. Louis, MO.

Chapter 3

1. Martin E. Lundi, "Effective Listening," *Guidelines on How to Conduct a Witness Workshop* (St. Louis: Board for Evangelism Services, The Lutheran Church—Missouri Synod, n.d.), pp. 57–64.
2. Miles, p. 101.
3. Haugk, pp. 150ff.
4. Flavil R. Yeakley, "The Friendship Factor," *Church Growth American* 8, no. 1 (January-February 1982).
5. Available from Concordia Tract Mission, Box 201, St. Louis, MO 63166.
6. Our Savior Lutheran Church, Bettendorf, Iowa.
7. Francis Matranga, *The Perfect Friend* (St. Louis: Concordia Publishing House, 1985), p. 69.
8. Haugk, pp. 150ff.
9. Ibid.

Chapter 4

1. "Evangelistic Gains and Inactive Losses of the American Lutheran Church," unpublished paper summarizing research (Minneapolis: American Lutheran Church, 1982).
2. John P. O'Hara, "Recent Data on 'Unchurched' Lutherans: Implications for Outreach Ministry" (Paper delivered to The Lutheran Church—Missouri Synod, St. Louis, October 1984).
3. Ibid.
4. Edwin T. Brown, "Some Witnessing Ideas for Daily Experiences," *The Reporter* (September 13, 1982).
5. Haugk, p. 126.
6. Nicolas Herman (Brother Lawrence), *The Practice of the Presence of God* (New York: Fleming H. Revell, 1985), p. 8. As quoted by Cecil Murphy, *Prayerobics* (Waco: Word Books, 1979), p. 22.
7. Lundi, p. 59.
8. *Guidelines on How to Conduct a Witness Workshop* (St. Louis: Board for Evangelism Services, The Lutheran Church—Missouri Synod, n.d.), p. 35.
9. Kenneth A. Erickson, *Please, Lord, Untie My Tongue* (St. Louis: Concordia Publishing House, 1983). Other helpful booklets:

   My Witness, A Series of Eight Study Booklets (Minneapolis: Augsburg, 1982.)

   Sixteen-page booklets from the ALC, some with very helpful material and others with less helpful materials for witness:

   "My Witness in Crisis Situations" by Elmer Laursen
   "How to Witness in Everyday Situations" by Fernanda Malmin
   "My Witness to the Face of Hostility" by Alvin C. Reuter
   "My Witness to Those Close to Me" by Leonard C. Erickson
   "My Witness to the Electronic Church" by Verle Reinicke
   "My Witness to a Contrary Witness" by Richard A. Jensen
   "My Witness to Those of Another Culture" by Paul Wee

10. Win and Charles Arn, *The Master's Plan for Making Disciples* (Pasadena, Calif.: Church Growth Press, 1982).
11. Ibid., p. 75.

12. Kenneth Scott Latourette, *A History of the Expansion of Christianity* (New York: Harper, 1937), vol. 1, *The First Five Centuries*, p. 116.
13. Ibid., p. 43.
14. Ibid.
15. *Information*, Lutheran World Federation, April 28, 1983.

Chapter 5
1. Elmer Kettner, *Adventures in Evangelism* (St. Louis: Concordia Publishing House, 1964), p. 29.
2. Strommen, *A Study of Generations.*
3. Ibid., p. 183.
4. Carl F. Reuss, *Profiles of Lutherans in the U.S.A.* (Minneapolis: Augsburg Publishing House, 1982). Questions taken from John O'Hara, *Profiles of Lutherans: A Study of Selected Characteristics and Attitudes of Lutherans in the United States* (Unpublished manuscript, 1980).
5. As quoted in Oscar E. Feucht, *Everyone a Minister* (St. Louis: Concordia Publishing House, 1974), p. 34.
6. Arthur M. Vincent, *The Christian Witness* (New York: American Lutheran Publicity Bureau, n.d.), p. 12.
7. Paul J. Foust, *Reborn to Multiply* (St. Louis: Concordia Publishing House, 1973), p. 16.
8. Ibid.
9. Merton P. Strommen, "A Compelling Need Among Us" (Essay published by the Affiliation of Lutheran Movements, 1982), pp. 1–20.
10. Ibid.
11. Kettner, pp. 122–23.
12. Leonard C. Erickson, "My Witness to Those Close to Me," My Witness Series (Minneapolis: Augsburg Publishing House, 1981), pp. 8–10.
13. Feucht, pp. 74–77.
14. Harvie M. Conn, *Evangelism: Doing Justice and Preaching Grace* (Grand Rapids: Zondervan Publishing House, 1982), p. 10.
15. Concordia Tract Mission, Box 201, St. Louis, MO 63166.

Chapter 6
1. Karl Menninger, *Whatever Became of Sin?* (New York: Hawthorne Books, Inc., 1973).
2. Gene A. Getz, *Sharpening the Focus of the Church* (Chicago: Moody Press, 1974), pp. 31–35.
3. Richard Stoll Armstrong, *The Pastor as Evangelist* (Philadelphia: Westminster Press, 1984), p. 22.
4. J. D. Douglas, ed., *Let the Earth Hear His Voice* (Minneapolis: World Wide Publication, 1975), p. 4.
5. W. H. Wente, "Conversion," *The Abiding Word*, ed. Theodore Laetsch (St. Louis: Concordia Publishing House, 1947), 1:182.
6. Ewald M. Plass, "Synergism," *The Abiding Word*, ed. Theodore Laetsch (St. Louis: Concordia Publishing House, 1947), 2:307.
7. *A Short Explanation of Dr. Martin Luther's Small Catechism* (St. Louis: Concordia Publishing House, 1943), p. 11.
8. *The Book of Concord: The Confessions of the Evangelical Lutheran Church,*

trans. and ed. Theodore G. Tappert in collaboration with Jaroslav Pelikan, Robert H. Fischer, and Arthur C. Piepkorn (Philadelphia: Fortress Press, 1959), p. 521.

9. Kettner, p. 63.

10. Arthur M. Vincent, "The Christmas Witness," reprinted from the *American Lutheran* (New York: American Lutheran Publicity Bureau, n.d.)

11. Kettner, p. 99.

12. Ibid.

13. D. James Kennedy, *Evangelism Explosion*, 3d ed. (Wheaton, Ill.: Tyndale House Publishers, 1983), p. 43.

14. W. Leroy Biesenthal, *Dialog Evangelism* (St. Louis: Board for Evangelism Services, The Lutheran Church—Missouri Synod, n.d.), pp. 64ff.

15. Richard G. Korthals, *Agape Evangelism: Roots That Reach Out* (Wheaton, Ill.: Tyndale House Publishers, 1980).

16. Robert Preus, "What Is Conversion?" *Lutheran Witness* 80 (August 8, 1961), p. 376.

Chapter 7

1. Michael J. Stelmachowicz, "The Power of Personal Witness," *Lutheran Witness* 102 (May 1983), p. 158.

2. John P. O'Hara, "Recent Data on 'Unchurched' Lutherans: Implications for Outreach Ministry."

3. *1980 Churches and Church Membership* (Washington: Glenmary Foundation, 1981).

4. O'Hara, p. 2.

5. Donald A. Abdon, *Training and Equipping the Saints* (Indianapolis: Parish Leadership Seminars, 1977).

6. Niles, *Overcoming Barriers to Witnessing*, p. 105.

7. C. Peter Wagner, *On the Crest of the Wave: Becoming a World Christian* (Ventura, Calif.: Regal Books, 1983).

Bibliography

Evangelism and Church Growth

Aldrich, Joseph C. *Life-Style Evangelism: Crossing Traditional Boundaries to Reach the Unbelieving World*. Portland: Multnomah Press, 1981. 246 pages.
Specific suggestions on how to witness to neighbors and friends through "incarnational/relational" evangelism.

Arn, Win, and Charles Arn, *The Master's Plan for Making Disciples*. Pasadena, Calif.: Church Growth Press, 1982. 176 pages.
The principles of making disciples through natural networks (webs) of friends and relatives.

Biesenthal, W. Leroy. *Dialog Evangelism*. St. Louis: Board for Evangelism Services, The Lutheran Church—Missouri Synod, 1980. 198 pages.
A Lutheran method of training callers to present the Gospel in home visitations using some of the "Kennedy" principles.

Erickson, Kenneth A. *Please, Lord, Untie My Tongue*. St. Louis: Concordia Publishing House, 1983. 63 pages.
Help in what to say to a person who is affected by illness, death, divorce, or imprisonment.

Feucht, Oscar E. *Everyone a Minister*. St. Louis: Concordia Publishing House, 1974. Paperback, 158 pages.
Presents the priesthood of all Christians as the only adequate strategy for the church, offering practical implications and applications.

Foust, Paul J., and Richard G. Korthals, *Reach Out: Evangelism for the Joy of It*. St. Louis: Concordia, 1984. 95 pages.
A book to challenge and motivate Christians to be the witnesses God intends them to be as part of His "building plan."

Foust, Paul J. *Reborn to Multiply*. St. Louis: Concordia, 1973. 56 pages.
Suggestions from a pastor and district executive in training lay people in evangelism and follow-up, based on personal experience.

Harre, Alan F. *Close the Back Door: Ways to Create a Caring Congregational Fellowship*. St. Louis: Concordia, 1984. 127 pages.
A description of the problem of the inactive member and dropout with a suggested program of training callers to visit inactives.

Haugk, Kenneth C. *Christian Caregiving: A Way of Life*. Minneapolis: Augsburg Publishing House, 1984. 157 pages.
The founder and director of the Stephen program provides help in training lay people to be "caregivers," which involves many witnessing skills such as listening and verbalizing the Gospel.

Heck, Joel D. *Make Disciples: Evangelism Programs of the Eighties*. St. Louis: Concordia, 1984. 111 pages.
A description and evaluation of a wide variety of evangelism programs with suggestions on how to determine whether they are appropriate for use in

a particular congregation.

Kettner, Elmer A. *Adventure in Evangelism.* St. Louis: Concordia Publishing House, 1964. 133 pages.

Directed to lay people, this book suggests ways to witness and provides many personal examples of witnessing. Out of print.

Kolb, Robert. *Speaking the Gospel Today: A Theology for Evangelism.* St. Louis: Concordia, 1984. 223 pages.

A Reformation scholar provides the theological basis for applying the Gospel to human need so that it heals and transforms.

Korthals, Richard G. *Agape Evangelism: Roots that Reach Out.* Wheaton, Ill.: Tyndale House, 1980. 219 pages.

A book by a Missouri Synod layman that helps the person who is learning the *Evangelism Explosion* style of evangelism with helpful suggestions and personal illustrations, all with an emphasis on *agape.*

Lieske, Bruce J. *Witnessing to Jewish People.* St. Louis: Board for Evangelism Services, The Lutheran Church—Missouri Synod, 1975; rev. 1984. 90 pages.

The best brief summary available about what Jewish people believe, anti-Semitism, and how to witness to Jews today.

Lischer, Richard. *Speaking of Jesus: Finding the Words for Witness.* Philadelphia: Fortress Press, 1982. 121 pages.

A Missouri Synod pastor offers suggestions for finding the words to speak as one witnesses with his life in personal relationships.

McPhee, Arthur G. *Friendship Evangelism: The Caring Way to Share Your Faith.* Grand Rapids, Mich.: Zondervan, 1978, 1980. 141 pages.

The radio speaker of the "Mennonite House" suggests ways for lay people to build relationships and then to share their faith.

Miles, Delos. *Overcoming Barriers to Witnessing.* Nashville: Broadman Press, 131 pages.

A Southern Baptist professor tackles 12 "barriers" that prevent Christians from witnessing, speaking from his own personal experiences and from his reading in the field.

Mueller, Charles S. *The Strategy of Evangelism.* St. Louis: Concordia Publishing House, 1965. 96 pages.

This book is intended as a "primer" by which a congregational evangelism committee can organize its outreach into the community.

My Witness, A Series of Eight Study Booklets. Minneapolis: Augsburg, 1982.

Sixteen-page booklets, some with very helpful material and others with less helpful material for witnessing:

"My Witness in Crisis Situations" by Elmer Laursen

"How to Witness to Humanists" by Lowell H. Mays

"How to Witness in Everyday Situations" by Fernanda Malmin

"My Witness to the Face of Hostility" by Alvin C. Reuter

"My Witness to Those Close to Me" by Leonard C. Erickson

"My Witness to the Electronic Church" by Verle Reinicke

"My Witness to a Contrary Witness" by Richard A. Jensen

"My Witness to Those of Another Culture" by Paul Wee

Rudnick, Milton L. *Speaking the Gospel Through the Ages: A History of Evangelism.* St. Louis: Concordia, 1984. 232 pages.

An interesting account of how people came to faith in Christ through the centuries from the 1st to the 20th.

Ulbrich, Armand. *Presenting the Gospel: How to Do So with Confidence and Joy.* St. Louis: Board of Evangelism, The Lutheran Church—Missouri Synod, 1977. 192 pages.

A guide to help an individual develop a personal outline for presenting the Gospel. Many options are offered. Out of print.

Witness Workshop. St. Louis: Board for Evangelism Services, The Lutheran Church—Missouri Synod, 1982. 108 pages.

A "how-to" manual for conducting a Witness Workshop to help people learn how to witness in their daily lives in a natural way.

Notes _____